I0796534

"Earth is the cradle of humanity, but one cannot live in a cradle forever."

Konstantin Tsiolkovsky, father of astronautics

Moving to MARS

Building a Colony on the Red Planet

Eduard Altarriba, Guillem Anglada-Escudé, Sheddad Kaid-Salah Ferrón & Miquel Sureda Anfres

BUTTON BOOKS

INTRODUCTION

Humans are curious animals. The desire for knowledge and search for new resources has pushed us to climb mountains, conquer the poles, and cross vast oceans. This tireless quest has even taken us into space. We make rockets that propel us into Earth's orbit and allow us to leave our mark on the Moon.

Far beyond, the final frontier awaits: Mars.

Mars, the so-called "Red Planet," is our unavoidable destiny if we want to become a multi-planetary species, living not just on Earth but on many planets. Settling on Mars will be a long process, starting with small scientific bases hidden among craters and ending with huge cities which can sustain themselves.

What will the journey from Earth to Mars be like? What will we find when we land? Where will we get oxygen and food? In this book you'll find the answers to many questions about what everyday life would be like in a Martian city.

DARE TO COME WITH US ON THE GREATEST ADVENTURE OF ALL!

MYTHS

The Romans named the planet Mars after their god of war, because of its blood-red color. The god Mars (known as Ares to the Greeks) represented violence, passion, and cruelty. Roman warriors worshipped him because they believed he would lead them to victory.

火星

מאדים

As humans explored (and exploited) our own planet and began to understand the vastness of the universe, we started to imagine what other life-forms might exist in space and on Mars, the planet most similar to ours. Maybe we sensed how strange and lonely it would be if Earth were the only planet in the universe with life.

We began to tell stories about Mars through books, pictures, comics, movies, and even scientific theories, turning it into a mirror for our hopes and fears. As we have studied and got to know the Red Planet, these stories have changed. Nowadays, no one expects to meet little green men on Mars. But finding past or present life-forms continues to be one of our main aims.

MARS AND EARTH: SISTER PLANETS

Of all the planets in the solar system, Mars is the most like Earth. It is a rocky planet; it has two permanent ice caps at its poles; the length of its days is almost identical to Earth's; and so too is the tilt of its rotational axis (the imaginary line from one pole to the other, about which it rotates).

Despite the similarities between the two planets, Mars also has some differences that would make it quite challenging to live there. The most important ones are its low average temperature, lack of liquid water on the surface, thin atmosphere, lack of oxygen, weak magnetic field, and low gravity.

	SURFACE AREA	RADIUS	MASS	AVERAGE DISTANCE FROM THE SUN
MARS	56 million miles² 144 million km²	2,106 miles 3,390 km	0.70×10^{21} tons 0.64×10^{24} kg	142 million miles 228 million km
EARTH	197 million miles² 510 million km²	3,963 miles 6,378 km	6.58×10^{21} tons 5.97×10^{24} kg	93 million miles 150 million km

AVERAGE TEMPERATURE	SOLAR DAY	YEAR	SURFACE GRAVITY
		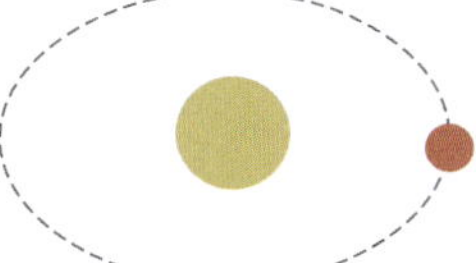	
−85°F −65°C	24 hours and 37 minutes *We call a Martian day a sol.*	668.6 Martian sols	12.1 ft/s^2 3.7 m/s^2
		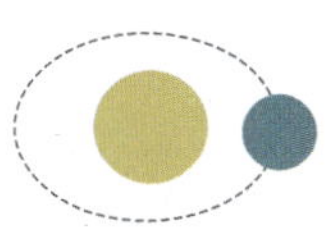	
59°F 15°C	23 hours and 56 minutes	365 Earth days	32.1 ft/s^2 9.8 m/s^2

PHOBOS AND DEIMOS

Mars's gravity keeps its two moons, Phobos and Deimos, in its orbit. It also deforms them slightly through what are known as "tidal forces." Due to the effect of these forces, Phobos and Deimos always show the same face to Mars, just as our moon always shows the same face to Earth.

PHOBOS

This small rock has an average radius of around 7 miles (11 km) and orbits Mars at a very high speed—in fact, it moves around the planet faster than Mars itself rotates!

Phobos's orbit is very close to Mars, about 3,700 miles (6,000 km) from the surface. This closeness, together with tidal forces, is causing Phobos's orbiting speed to gradually decrease, or decelerate. As a result of this, it is estimated that Phobos will eventually collide with Mars in 50 million years. That is, if it doesn't disintegrate first.

The Stickney crater is about 5.6 miles (9 km) wide, a little less than Phobos's radius.

In 1877, American astronomer Asaph Hall discovered Mars's two small moons. He called them Phobos (fear) and Deimos (terror) after the twin sons that the Greek god Ares (Mars) had with Aphrodite, the goddess of beauty and love. The twins always accompanied their father into battle.

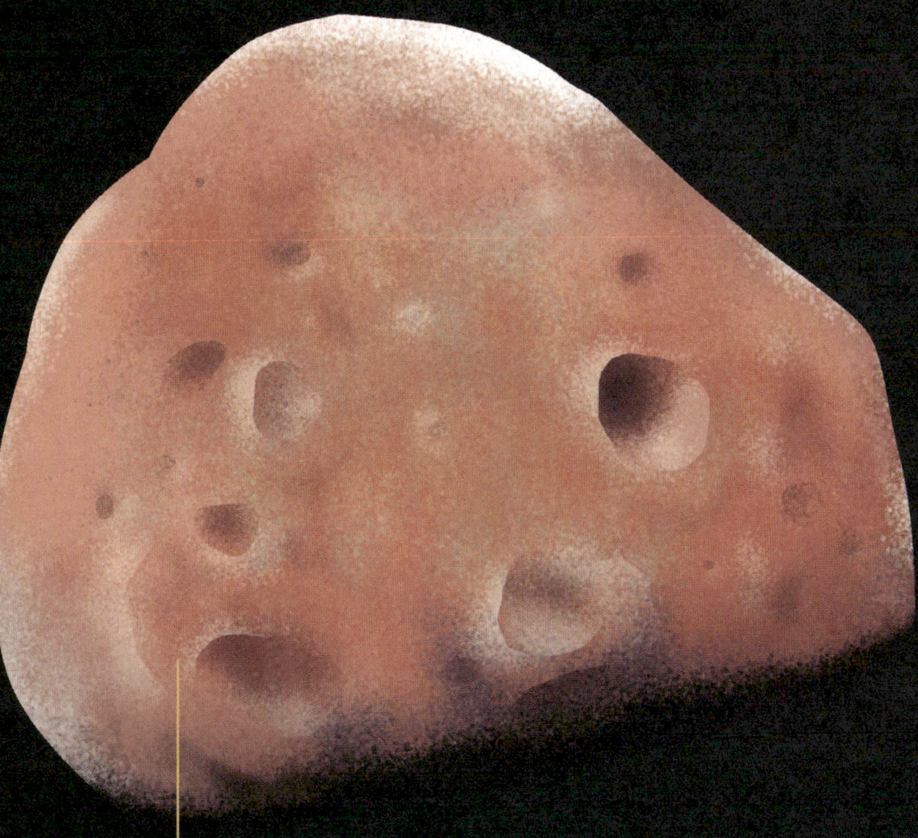

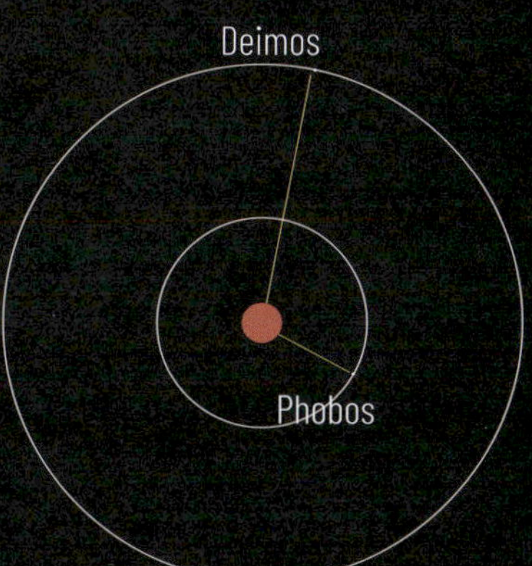

DEIMOS

Smaller and farther out than Phobos, Deimos has an average radius of around 3.8 miles (6 km).

Mars's two satellites are so small, they are little more than dots in the Martian sky.

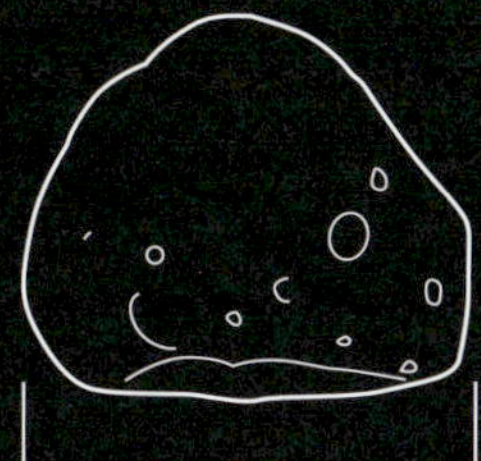

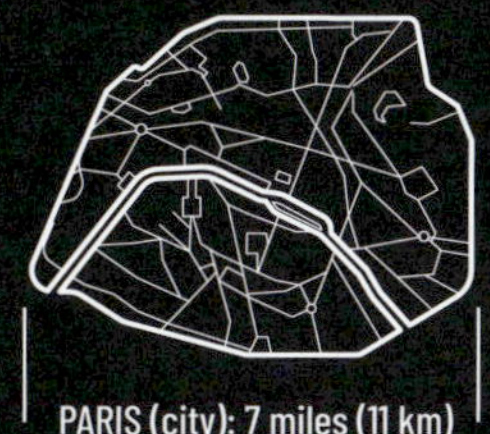

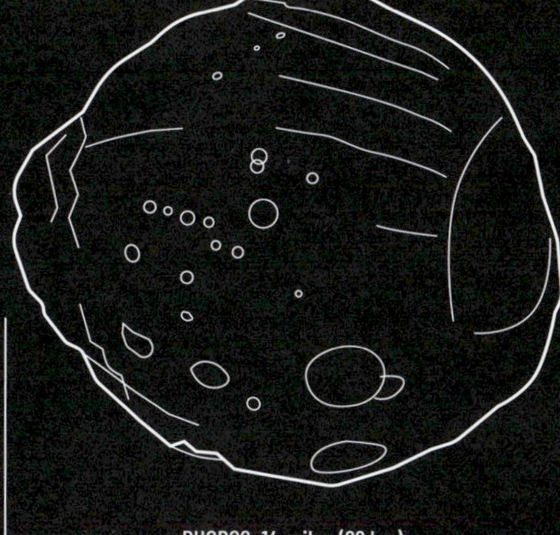

THE MOON:
2,160 miles (3,476 km)

Space exploration presents a number of huge challenges. No sooner have we left the safety of our planet than we come face to face with two of the universe's greatest threats: solar wind and cosmic radiation.

SOLAR WIND

Solar wind is a stream of very high-energy particles (basically protons, electrons, and alpha particles) that are released from the solar corona, the Sun's upper atmosphere. Solar wind is extremely harmful and dangerous for living beings.

Sometimes the Sun can release a larger quantity of very high-energy particles. These are the extremely dangerous solar storms. Luckily, this doesn't happen very often.

Our solar system revolves around a single star, the Sun, whose enormous gravity is so powerful that it holds the planets in orbit around it.

The Sun is a large hot sphere of plasma, formed mainly of hydrogen (H) and helium (He). It is an ordinary star and there is nothing special about it—except, of course, that it is ours. It is what provides us with the energy needed for life on Earth.

The Sun is a yellow dwarf-type star. It is called "dwarf" because it is small compared to other bigger stars, and "yellow" because of the color of its surface. But although it is small, it is still nearly 865,000 miles (1.4 million km) in diameter. Over 1,000,000 Earths would fit inside it!

Due to nuclear fusion reactions, the inside of the Sun is very hot, around 27 million°F (15 million°C). However, its surface is much cooler, with a temperature of about 10,000°F (5,500°C).

THE MAGNETOSPHERE

The Earth's inner core is a liquid mass of molten iron and nickel. When it moves, it creates electric currents that produce a magnetic field. Earth acts like a giant magnet, with a magnetic north pole and south pole.

The magnetic field extends out from the center of Earth into space, creating a giant bubble of magnetism around our planet called the magnetosphere. This deflects most of the solar wind.

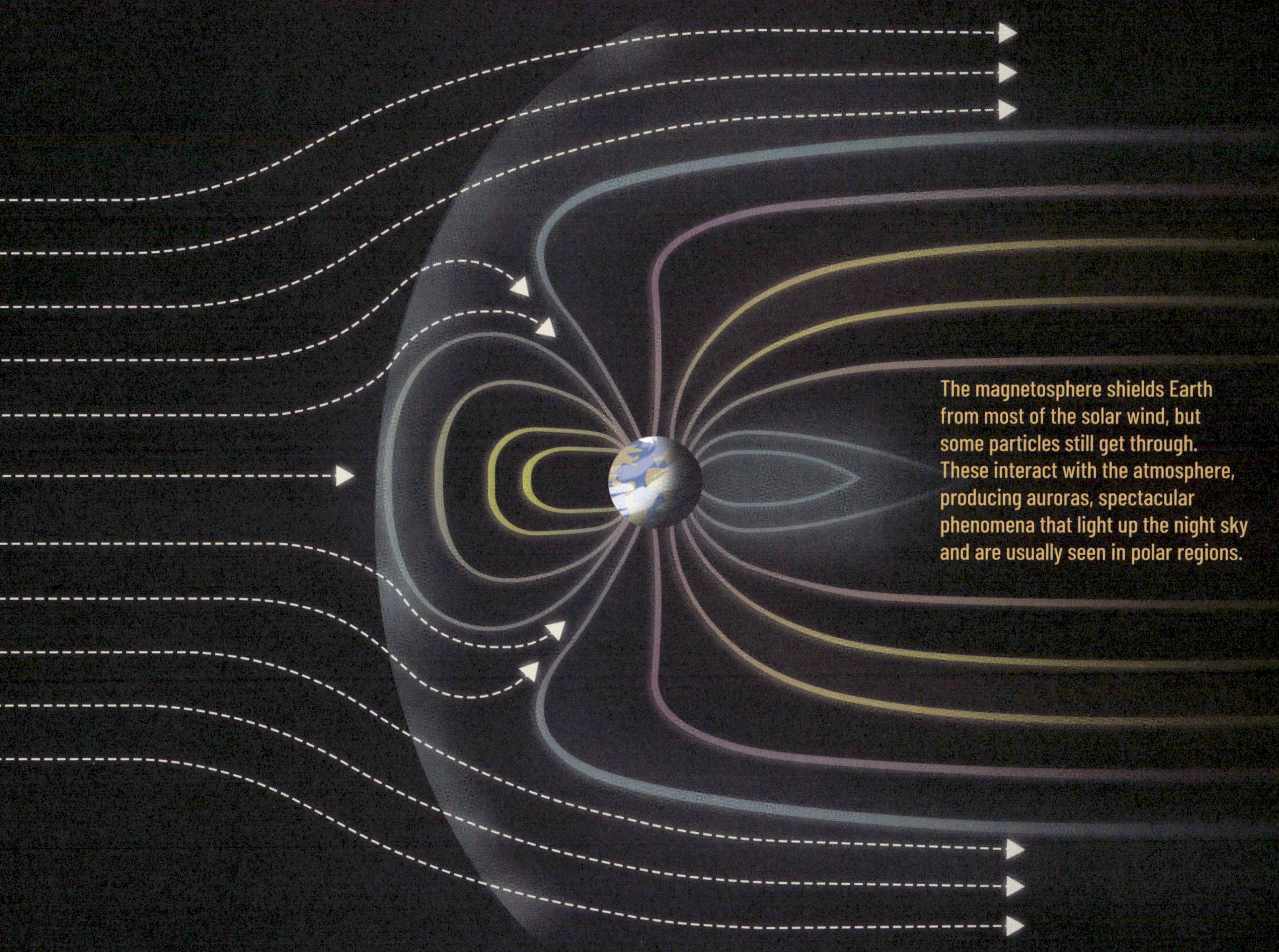

On a planet like Mars that only has traces of magnetism and doesn't have a magnetosphere, solar wind particles collide with particles in the atmosphere and drag them into outer space. This causes the atmosphere to gradually weaken until it decreases and almost disappears.

COSMIC RADIATION

Cosmic radiation, or cosmic rays, are mostly electrically charged particles from outer space that travel very fast (some almost at the speed of light), which makes them very high energy. These particles come from all directions and are extremely harmful to all life-forms—animals, plants, fungi, and microorganisms. This is because they can penetrate and even pass through organisms, damaging their cells.

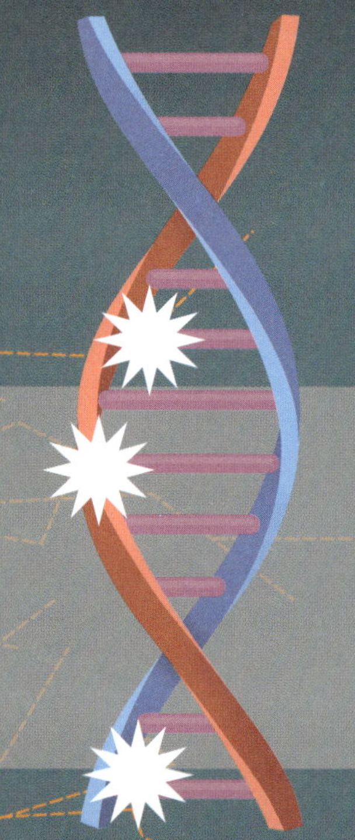

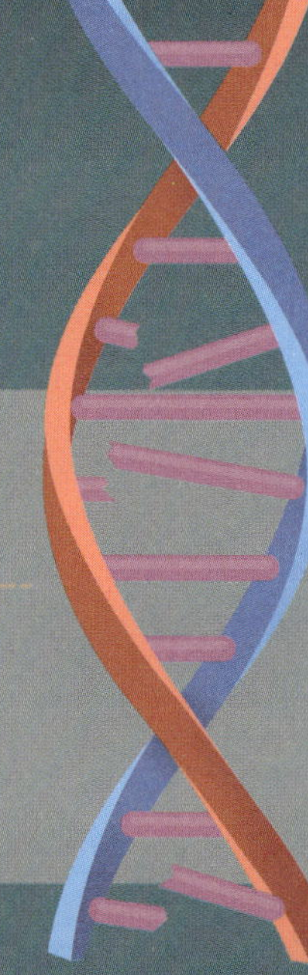

As cosmic radiation particles pass through cells, they can cause irreparable damage. As a result, the cells stop working normally and lose the ability to heal themselves.

Radiation is one of the main problems both for traveling to Mars and for settling there. Once astronauts have left Earth and its protective magnetosphere, they are exposed to very high doses of cosmic radiation and this can be lethal.

The magnetic field is our shield

The magnetosphere is the layer that the magnetic field forms around the Earth. It is a protective shield that shelters us from solar wind and cosmic radiation.

The Earth's magnetic field protects us from most of the particles that reach us. Very few of them interact with the atmosphere and make it to the Earth's surface. Without this protection, our planet would have hardly any atmosphere and there would be a lot of surface radiation: life would be much harder.

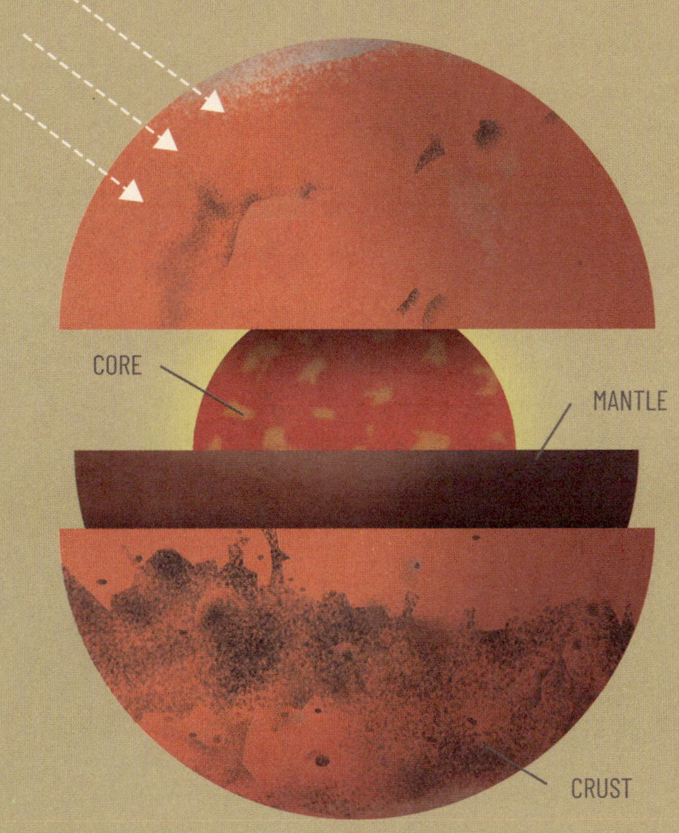

Unlike Earth, Mars has no magnetosphere to protect it from cosmic radiation and solar wind.

Shortly after Mars formed, it enjoyed similar conditions to those on Earth: it had a rotating molten iron core that could generate a magnetosphere. This protected Mars from cosmic radiation and solar wind and allowed it to have a stable atmosphere.

But because Mars is smaller than Earth, things changed over time. Mars's core, which is smaller than Earth's and has less energy, ended up cooling down about 4 billion years ago and practically stopped rotating. This meant Mars lost its ability to create a protective magnetic field.

THE ATMOSPHERE

The atmosphere is the layer of gases around a planet. The gases are attracted by the planet's gravity and, if it is strong enough, they become trapped. The weaker the gravity, the harder it is for the planet to keep hold of the particles that make up the gases in its atmosphere.

Mars's atmosphere, unlike Earth's, has a very thin layer of gases. It is about 100 times less dense than Earth's, making it very thin and light.

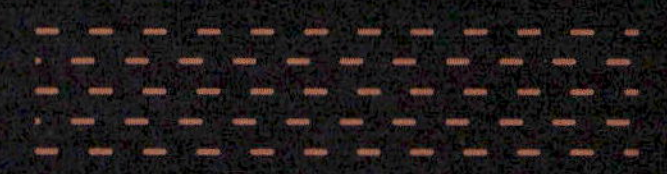

WHAT IS THE ATMOSPHERE MADE OF?

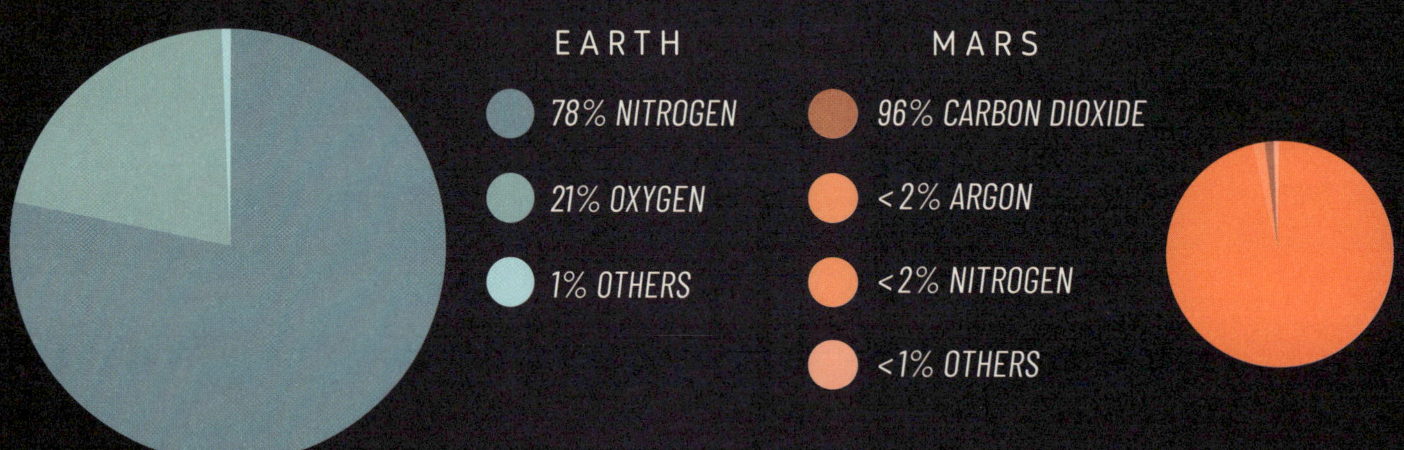

BREATHING ON MARS

Carbon dioxide (CO_2) is the most abundant gas on Mars. In high concentrations, it is poisonous to humans. It makes up about 0.04% of our atmosphere, but 96% of Mars's! Oxygen (O_2), which we need to breathe, is practically non-existent on Mars.

To survive on the surface of Mars, we will need spacesuits to protect us and to supply us with oxygen to breathe. Without the helmet and suit, we would suffocate and the low atmospheric pressure would cause our blood to boil . . . and these two things would happen at almost the same time!

Loss of atmosphere

Mars's atmosphere is slowly but steadily leaking into outer space. As it has no magnetosphere, solar wind particles collide with particles in its atmosphere, sending some of them flying off into space. Mars's atmosphere has decreased over time to a thin and light layer of gases.

The methane mystery

In 2004, the *Mars Express* probe detected methane gas (CH_4) in Mars's atmosphere. This came as a big surprise to the scientific community. On Earth, methane is produced partly by certain geological processes, but mainly by living things. Data from other missions have not explained how the methane on Mars is formed or destroyed. We will have to continue investigating and collecting information to solve the mystery.

CLIMATE

Compared to Earth, the climate on Mars is extreme. It is much colder and drier, with a big contrast in temperatures and huge dust storms that can cover the whole planet.

Modern rovers and landers on Mars have weather stations that provide us with information about the weather in different regions of the planet.

EXTREME DIFFERENCES

The difference between daytime and nighttime temperatures are very high.

In summer, on the equator, maximum daytime temperatures can reach 95°F (35°C), while minimum nighttime temperatures can easily drop to −112°F (−80°C). That's a difference of over 200°F (100°C)!

Although the planet's average temperature is −85°F (−65°C), surface temperatures vary from lows of around −225°F (−143°C) at the polar caps in winter, to highs of 95°F (35°C) on the equator in summer.

This big temperature difference is mainly due to the fact that the thin and weak atmosphere on Mars cannot hold much heat.

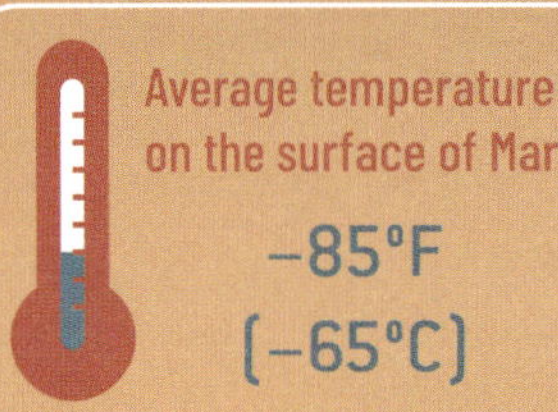

−225°F
(−143°C)

NORTHERN HEMISPHERE

EQUATOR

SOUTHERN HEMISPHERE

−225°F
(−143°C)

Temperature difference

The temperature difference between day and night in summer, on the equator, is more than 200°F (100°C)!

DAY
95°F
(35°C)

NIGHT
−112°F
(−80°C)

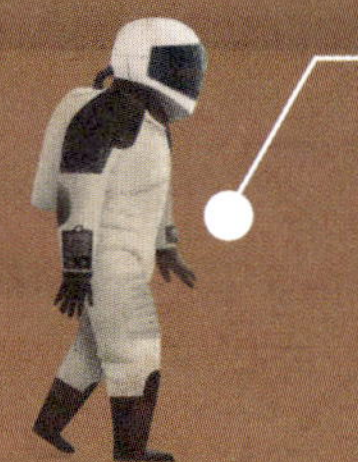

Spacesuits worn on the surface of Mars need to have an adjustable heating system.

The temperature difference between areas in the sun and the shade can be tens of degrees.

Seasons on Mars

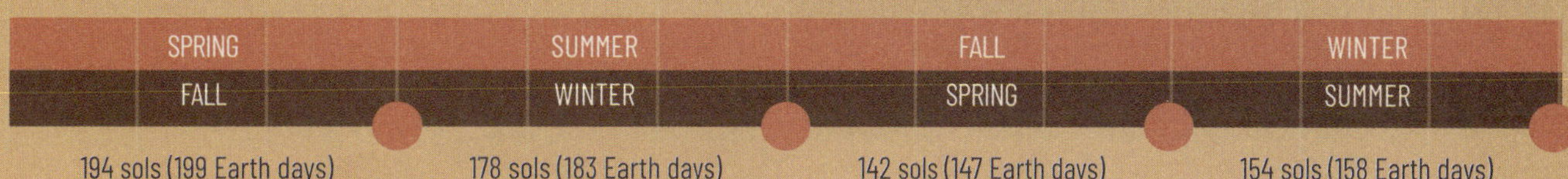

rtian year is equal to 3.6 sols or 687 Earth days.

194 sols (199 Earth days) | 178 sols (183 Earth days) | 142 sols (147 Earth days) | 154 sols (158 Earth days)

The tilt of Earth's and Mars's rotational axes, in relation to their orbits around the Sun, is very similar. This is why Mars, like Earth, has different seasons in the two hemispheres. When it is spring or summer in the northern hemisphere, it is fall or winter in the southern hemisphere, and vice versa.

Tilt of Mars's axis: 25 degrees

However, Mars's orbit is much less circular than Earth's (see page 22). Because its orbit is not a perfect circle, the distance from the Sun changes depending on Mars's position. This means seasons on Mars last for different amounts of time in the northern and southern hemispheres. In the northern hemisphere, spring and summer are longer than fall and winter.

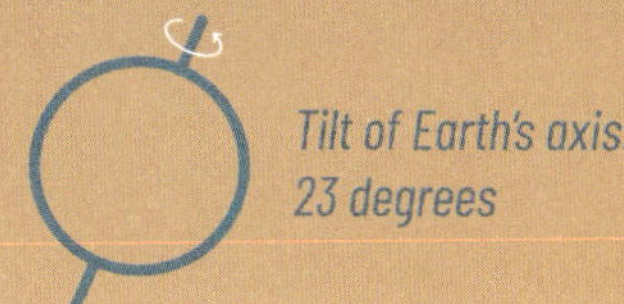

Tilt of Earth's axis: 23 degrees

Sandstorms

Mars experiences impressive sand and dust storms that can leave its surface totally covered for weeks or even months. It is one of the planet's major weather phenomena.

Dust particles on Mars are very small and light, and even a moderate wind can whip up clouds of dust. But the really spectacular storms come from the winds of up to 90 mph (150 km/h) that usually occur in late spring in the southern hemisphere. During this time, Mars is closer to the Sun and high temperatures cause the planet's surface to lose its moisture. Huge amounts of suspended dust create a yellow haze that turns the atmosphere dark and block out the Sun, making temperatures drop.

The whirlwinds of dust or "dust devils" are similar to tornados in deserts on Earth. They happen when the Sun heats up the ground and the air rises really fast, forming a column of air and dust that spins very quickly as it moves.

WATER

Life as we know it needs water to survive. Setting up a human settlement on Mars would be impossible without water, but the existence of water on the planet could also mean that in the past there was some form of life.

IN THE PAST

Mars's surface has long been dry and arid, but there is lots of evidence that it once had large amounts of liquid water and was home to seas, rivers, and streams.

Probes have found many signs of liquid water existing in the past—river beds, tributaries, and estuaries. Traces of these can be seen in the marks they have left on the planet's surface, caused by the action of water erosion.

An ancient river delta in the Jezero crater © NASA/JPL/JHUAPL/MSSS/Brown University

THE GREAT OCEAN OF MARS

In the Noachian Era (4.1 to 3.5 billion years ago), Mars had a dense atmosphere and a much milder average temperature. This meant it had liquid water permanently on its surface.

It is thought that around 4.1 billion years ago, there was a sea—known as the Oceanus Borealis—in the planet's northern hemisphere, which covered around 20% of the surface (almost two Atlantic Oceans). This would explain the difference between the northern hemisphere's smooth, flat surface and the southern hemisphere's rough, cratered surface.

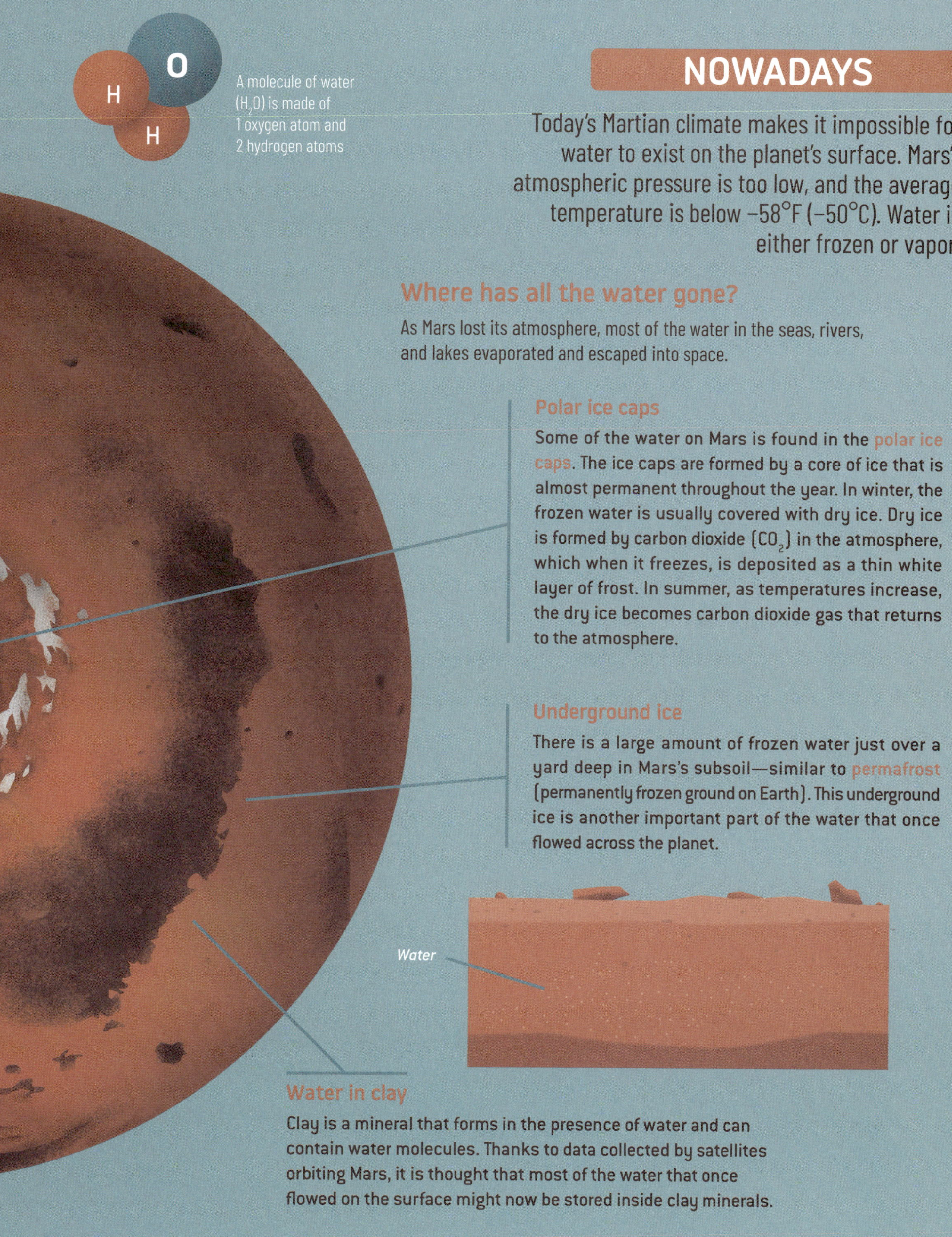

A molecule of water (H_2O) is made of 1 oxygen atom and 2 hydrogen atoms

NOWADAYS

Today's Martian climate makes it impossible for water to exist on the planet's surface. Mars's atmospheric pressure is too low, and the average temperature is below −58°F (−50°C). Water is either frozen or vapor.

Where has all the water gone?

As Mars lost its atmosphere, most of the water in the seas, rivers, and lakes evaporated and escaped into space.

Polar ice caps

Some of the water on Mars is found in the polar ice caps. The ice caps are formed by a core of ice that is almost permanent throughout the year. In winter, the frozen water is usually covered with dry ice. Dry ice is formed by carbon dioxide (CO_2) in the atmosphere, which when it freezes, is deposited as a thin white layer of frost. In summer, as temperatures increase, the dry ice becomes carbon dioxide gas that returns to the atmosphere.

Underground ice

There is a large amount of frozen water just over a yard deep in Mars's subsoil—similar to permafrost (permanently frozen ground on Earth). This underground ice is another important part of the water that once flowed across the planet.

Water in clay

Clay is a mineral that forms in the presence of water and can contain water molecules. Thanks to data collected by satellites orbiting Mars, it is thought that most of the water that once flowed on the surface might now be stored inside clay minerals.

A HARD-TO-REACH DESTINATION

Mars's nearness and similarity to Earth have made it the most studied planet in the solar system. However, missions to the Red Planet have not always been successful. Almost half have failed due to explosions on launch, probes lost in space, communication problems, or landers that have smashed into its surface.

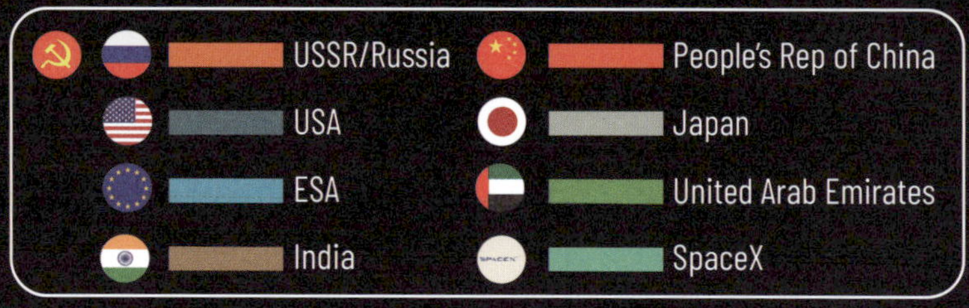

1960
MARS 1M (NO. 1)
MARS 1M (NO. 2)

1962
MARS 2MV-4 (NO. 1)
MARS 1
MARS 2MV-3 (NO. 1)

1964
MARINER 3
MARINER 4
ZOND 2

1969
MARINER 6
MARINER 7
MARS M-69 (NO. 521)
MARS M-69 (NO. 522)

1971
MARINER 8
KOSMOS 419
MARS 2
MARS 3
MARINER 9

1973
MARS 4
MARS 5
MARS 6
MARS 7

1975
VIKING 1
VIKING 2

1988
FOBOS 1
FOBOS 2

92
MARS OBSERVER

1996
MARS GLOBAL SURVEYOR
MARS 8 / MARS 96
MARS PATHFINDER

1998
NOZOMI
MARS CLIMATE ORBITER

99
MARS POLAR LANDER / DEEP SPACE 2

01
2001 MARS ODYSSEY

2003
MARS EXPRESS / BEAGLE 2
SPIRIT
OPPORTUNITY

05
MARS RECONAISANCE ORBITER

07
PHOENIX

2011
FOBOS-GRUNT & YINGHUO
CURIOSITY

2013
MARS ORBITER MISSION
MAVEN

16
EXOMARS 2016

18
INSIGHT

2020
EMIRATES MARS MISSION
TIANWEN-1
MARS 2020

FUTURE MISSIONS
ESCAPADE
MARS LANDER MISSION
TIANWEN-3
EXOMARS ROSALIND FRANKLIN
MARS SAMPLE RETURN
SPACEX UNCREWED LANDING
SPACEX FIRST CREWED LANDING

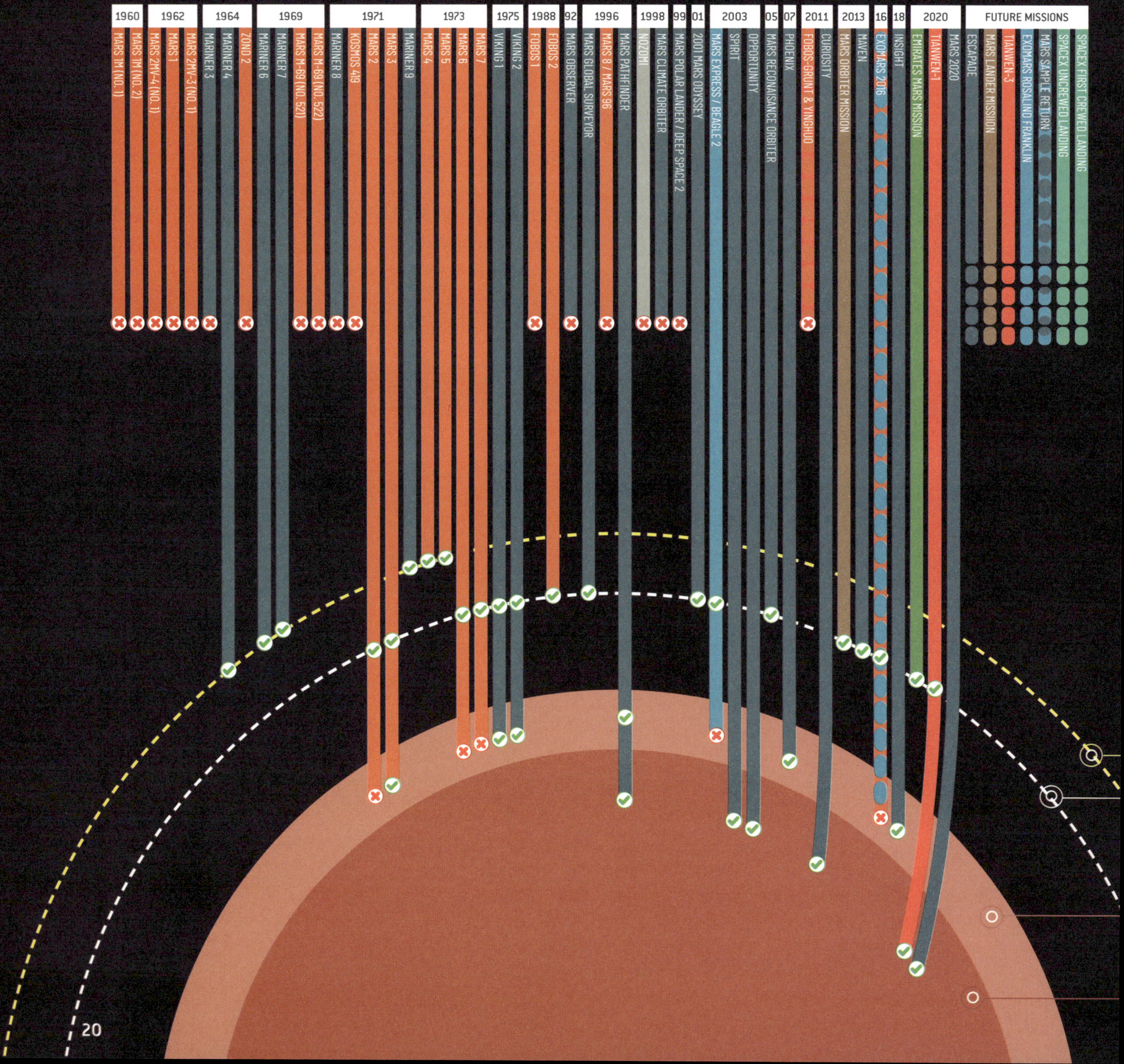

Flyby

A probe passes close to the planet to take pictures and collect scientific data during a short period of time, and then moves away without entering orbit.

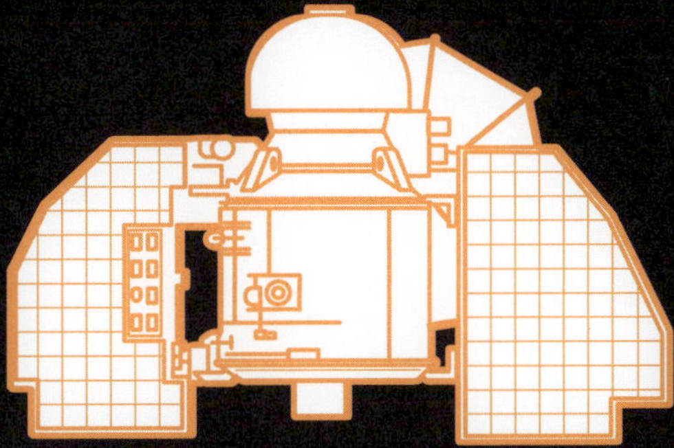

MARS 1M: FIRST MISSIONS TO MARS
USSR, 1960

Two spacecraft were launched on October 10th and 14th, 1960. Both craft were lost due to launch failures.

MARINER 4
USA, 1964

The first successful mission to Mars! It flew over the planet at a distance of 6,118 miles (9,846 km), taking 21 photographs of its surface.

Orbiter

A satellite enters orbit around Mars to take pictures, collect scientific data, and perform communications tasks.

MARS EXPRESS
Europe, 2003

The European Space Agency's (ESA) first mission to Mars, which included an orbiter and a lander (*Beagle 2*). The orbiter managed to take many photographs and collect scientific data, but *Beagle 2* failed to deploy properly after landing.

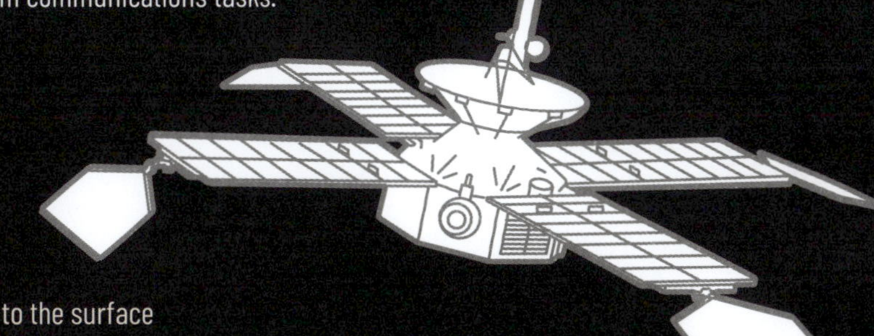

Lander

A landing module descends to the surface of Mars and stays where it landed to use its scientific instruments.

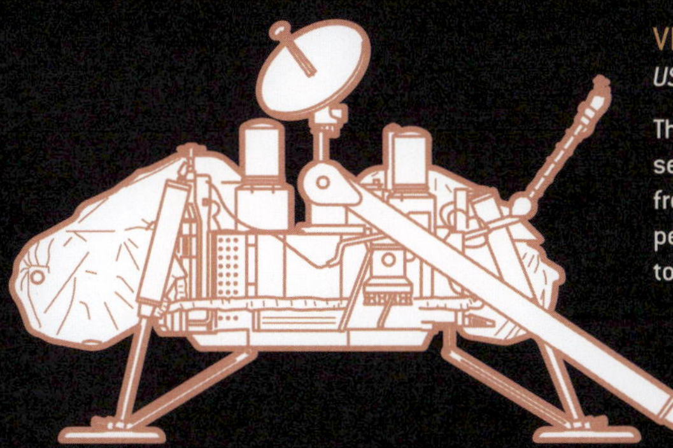

VIKING 1: FIRST SUCCESSFUL LANDING
USA, 1975

This landing module sent us the first images taken from the surface of Mars and performed experiments to search for signs of life.

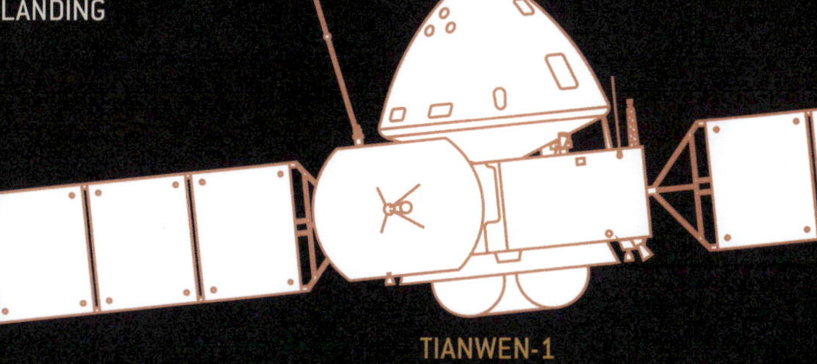

TIANWEN-1
China, 2020

This mission took an orbiter, a landing module, and a rover called *Zhurong* to Mars.

Rover

A rover lands on Mars's surface and moves around to perform experiments at different points in a particular area.

MARS PATHFINDER
USA, 1996

Sojourner was the first rover that could move autonomously (under its own control) on another planet.

INGENUITY

PERSEVERANCE

ROVERS

Modern rovers move around the surface of Mars doing complex experiments. These study whether there was life on Mars in the past and prepare for the technology that will be needed for future settlements. Some rovers have small drones capable of flying in the thin Martian atmosphere.

ORBITS

The orbits of planets around the Sun are elliptical, which means they are shaped like slightly squashed circles. Some are flatter and more squashed than others. Earth's orbit is almost circular. In contrast, Mars's orbit is quite flat; this is why the distance between the Sun and other planets (especially Mars) is NOT always the same, nor is the distance between Mars and Earth.

Inner solar system
1 AU
MERCURY
VENUS
EARTH
MARS
Asteroid belt
JUPITER
10 AU
SATURN
Outer solar system
URANUS
20 AU
NEPTUNE
30 AU
Pluto
40 AU

The sizes of planets are NOT to scale compared to the distances

The AU (Astronomical unit) is equivalent to the average distance between Earth and the Sun, around 93 million miles (150 million km).

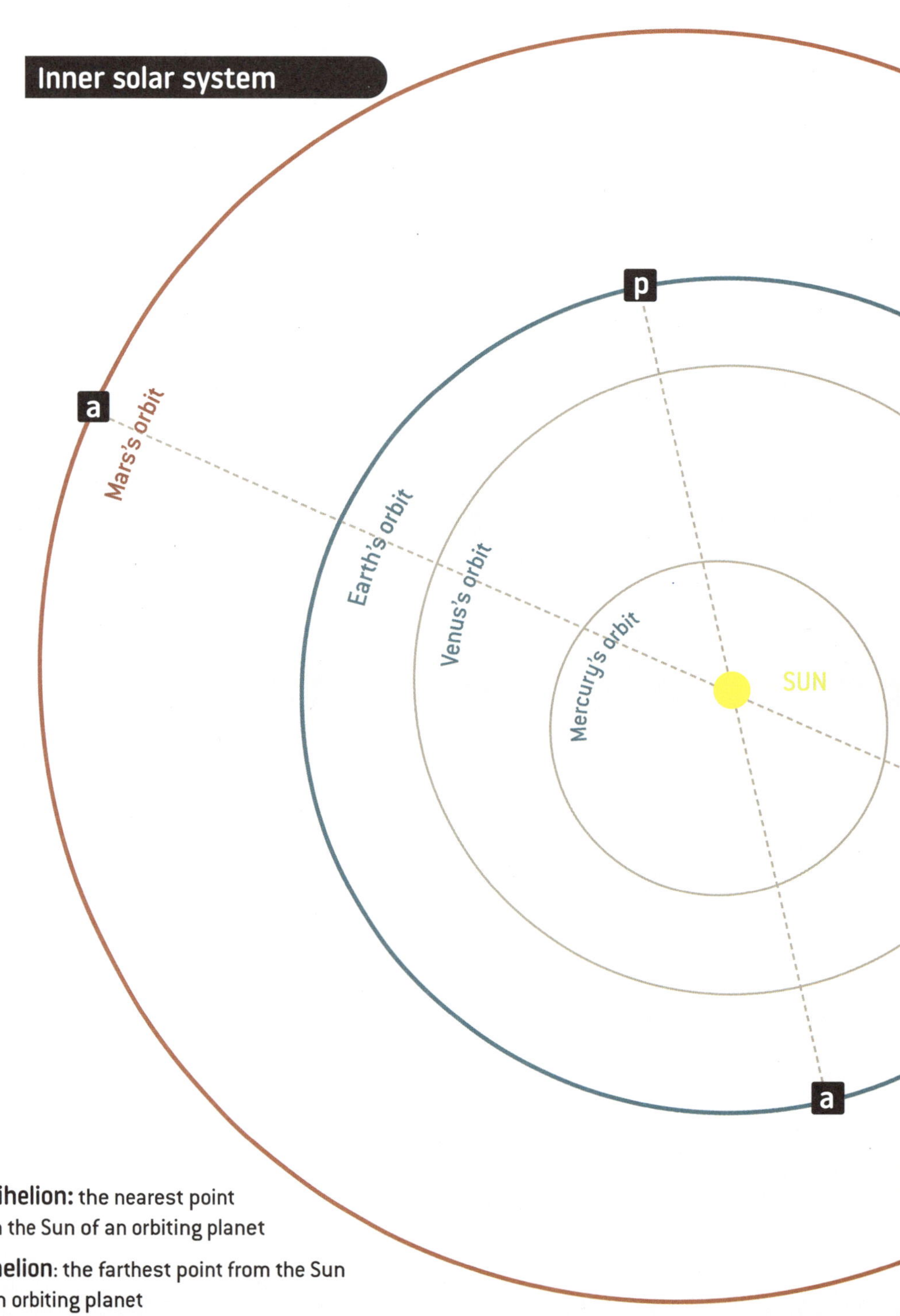

p Perihelion: the nearest point from the Sun of an orbiting planet

a Aphelion: the farthest point from the Sun of an orbiting planet

Orbital period:
Mars takes 687 Earth days to complete an orbit around the Sun, in other words, a Martian year is almost two Earth years. The distance between Mars and Earth varies a lot depending on where each planet is in its orbital cycle.

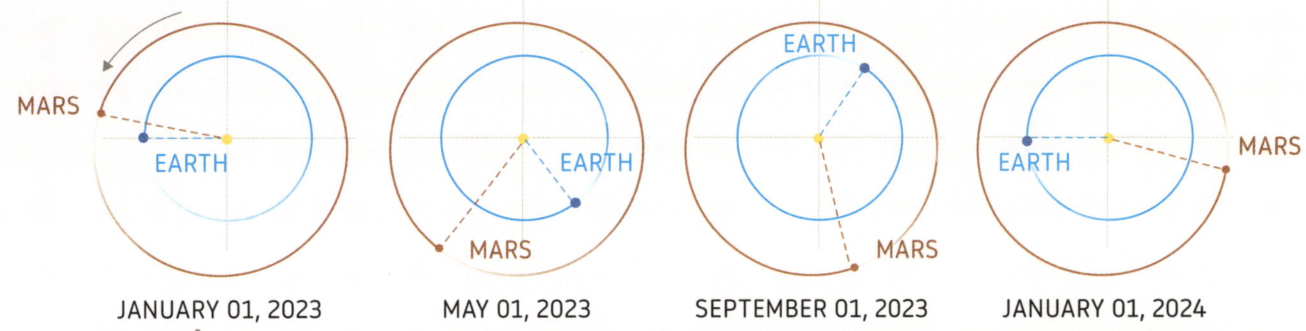

To see the rotation of planets, satellites, and asteroids in our solar system, visit: eyes.nasa.gov/apps/asteroids

MARS OPPOSITIONS

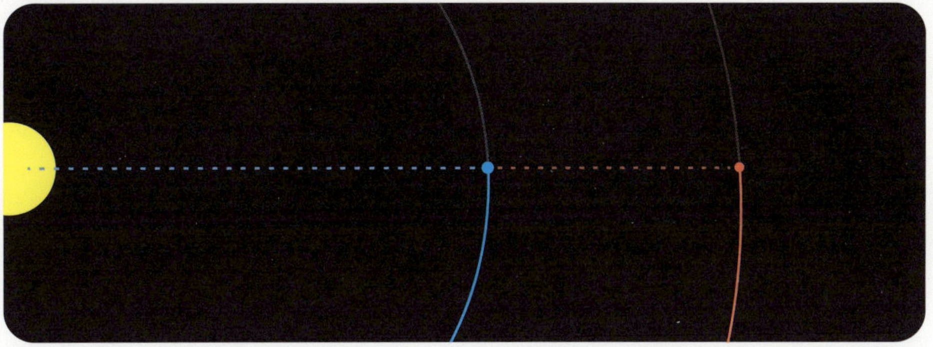

"Oppositions" are events that take place when Earth and Mars are in line with the Sun. They happen on average every 780 days (around 2 years and 2 months) and are the moment when the two planets are usually closest to one another.

Oppositions are ideal for observing Mars and are also the best time to launch missions to Mars, as this is when it is closest to Earth.

As the orbital periods of Earth and Mars are different, oppositions do not tend to take place at the same orbital points. This is why minimum distances between the two planets are not always the same.

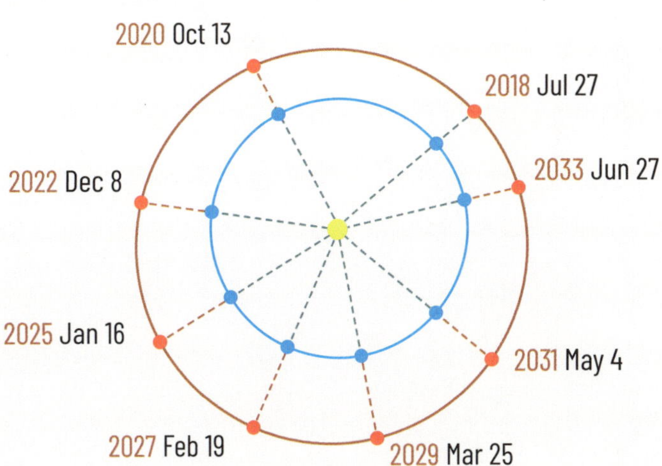

SOME ORBITAL MECHANICS

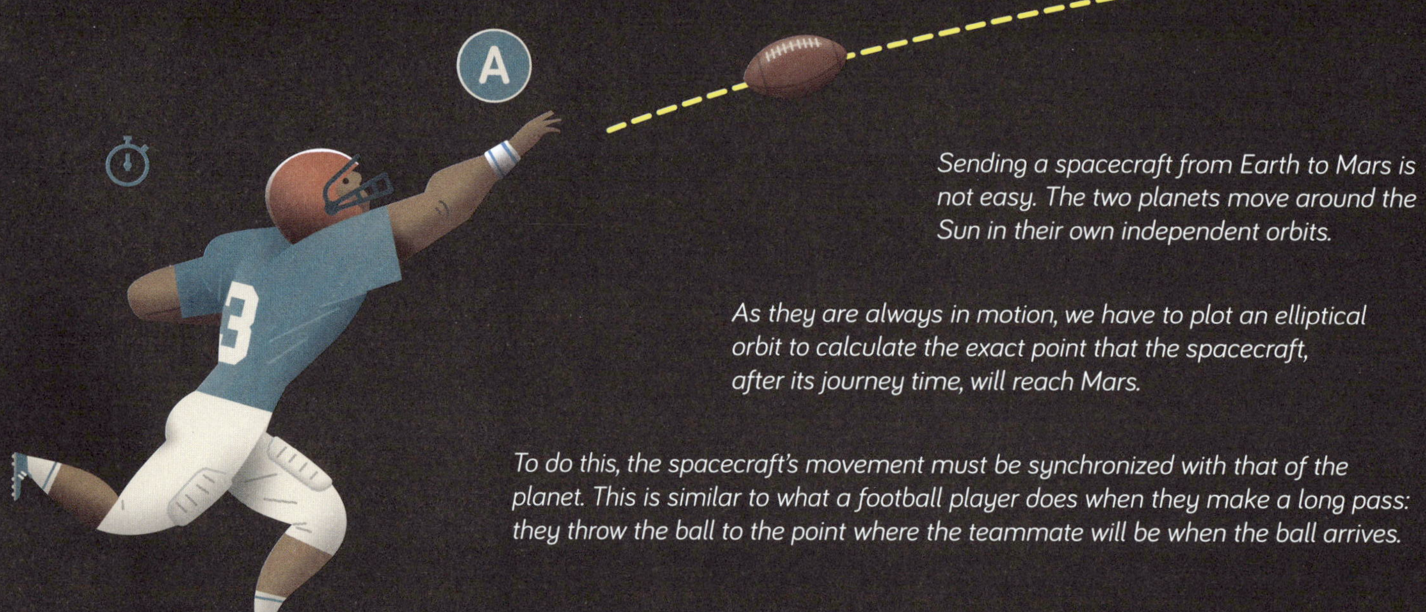

Sending a spacecraft from Earth to Mars is not easy. The two planets move around the Sun in their own independent orbits.

As they are always in motion, we have to plot an elliptical orbit to calculate the exact point that the spacecraft, after its journey time, will reach Mars.

To do this, the spacecraft's movement must be synchronized with that of the planet. This is similar to what a football player does when they make a long pass: they throw the ball to the point where the teammate will be when the ball arrives.

A trajectory is the curved path of an object as it moves through space. When we calculate the trajectory of a spacecraft between planets, we have to take into account the forces of gravity that will affect it. All planets have a zone around them, within which their gravity is stronger than the Sun's and controls the movement of passing bodies such as spacecraft. This zone is called the sphere of influence. When a spacecraft leaves this zone, the Sun's gravity becomes dominant instead.

Using today's technology, the time it takes a spacecraft from Earth to reach Mars varies between 200 and 300 days, depending on the spacecraft's speed and the distance between Earth and Mars at the time of launch.

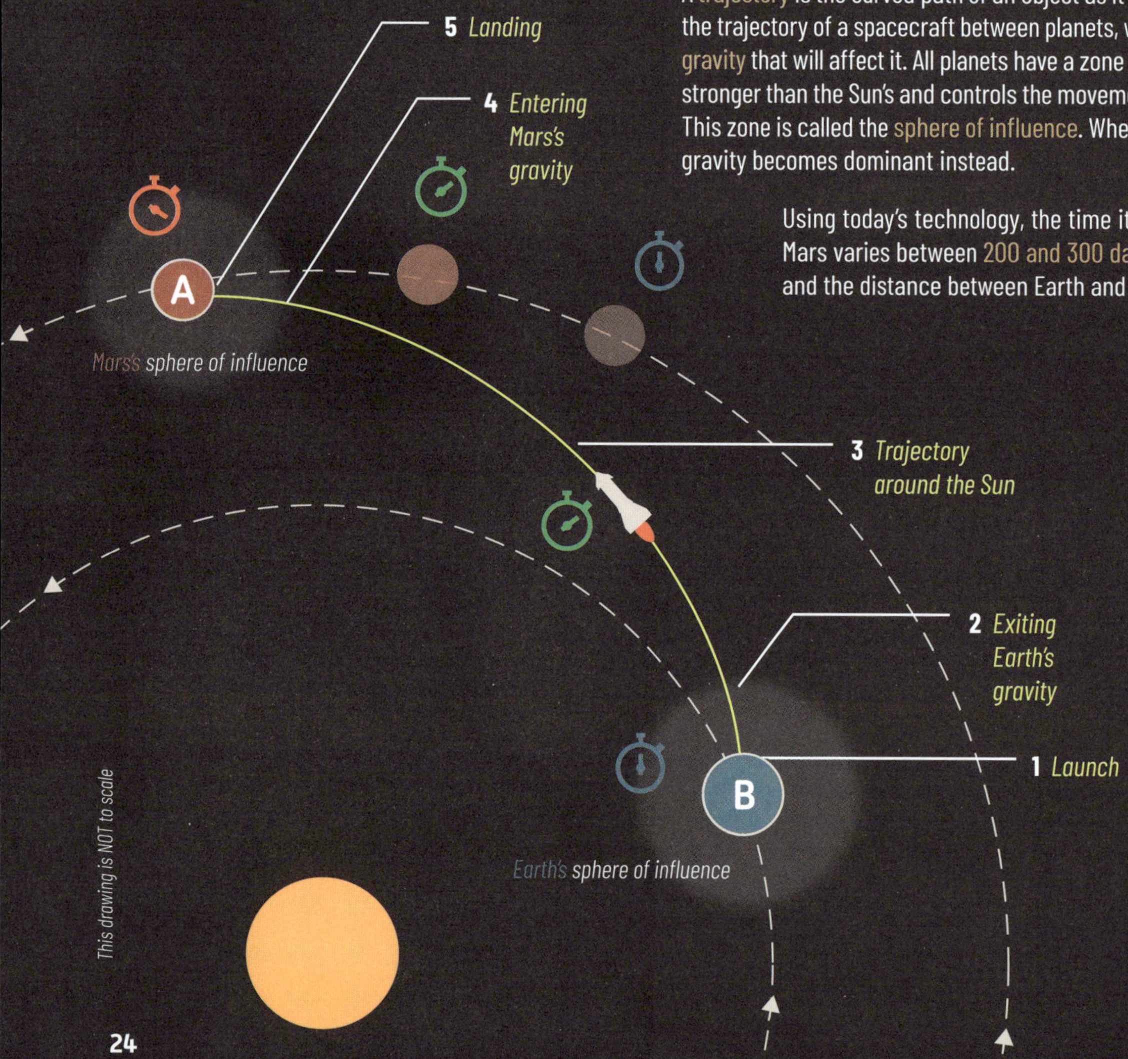

The journey to Mars cannot begin at just any time. It has to wait until the planets are close to their opposition (see page 23). This happens every 780 days (two years and two months), when there is a launch window that lasts up to a month.

Once a spacecraft escapes Earth's gravity and enters orbit around the Sun at the right speed, it does not need further propulsion from its engines to stay within that orbit—just like a football player only needs to propel the ball at the start of the throw. The engines are fired up only at the start and the end of the journey to Mars, apart from any small corrections to the orbit needed during the cruise.

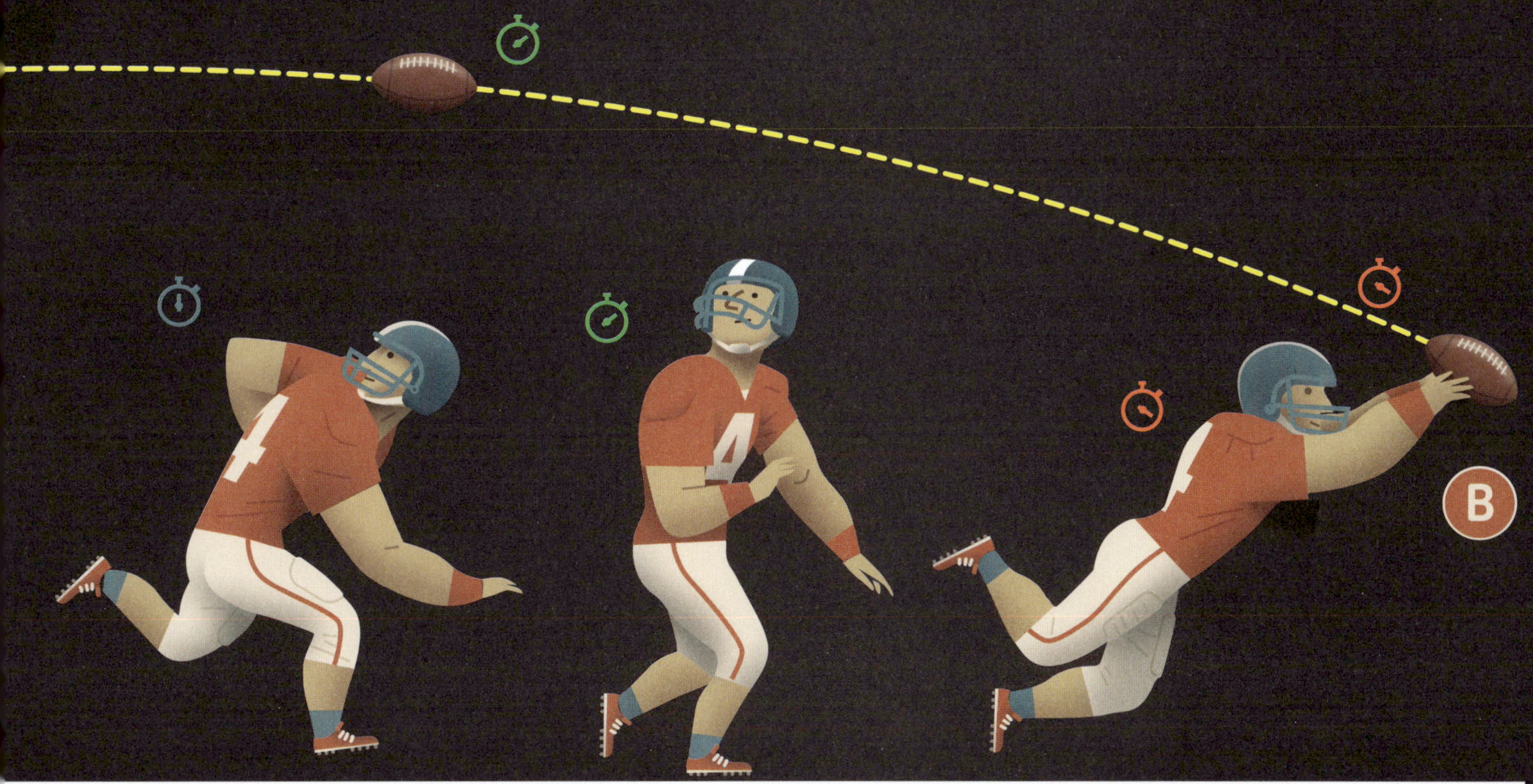

Conical trajectories

The orbits of bodies in space (spacecraft, asteroids, etc.) come in different geometric shapes, called conic sections. These can be circles, ellipses, parabolas, or hyperbolas, depending on each body's energy.

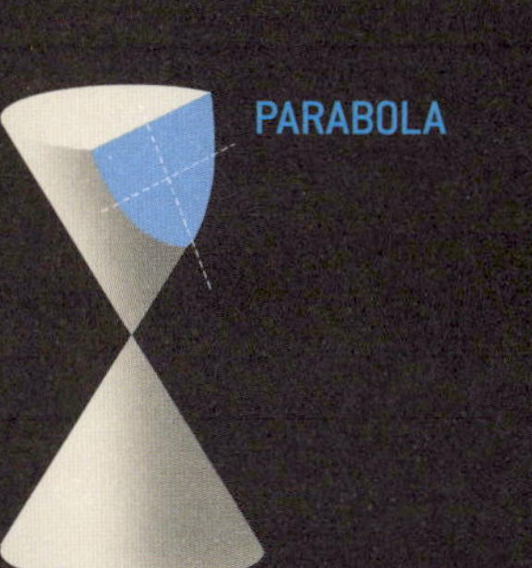

All these geometric shapes are found by slicing through a cone!

We use the different orbits to calculate the trajectory of bodies in space and the path that spacecraft need to follow to reach their destination.

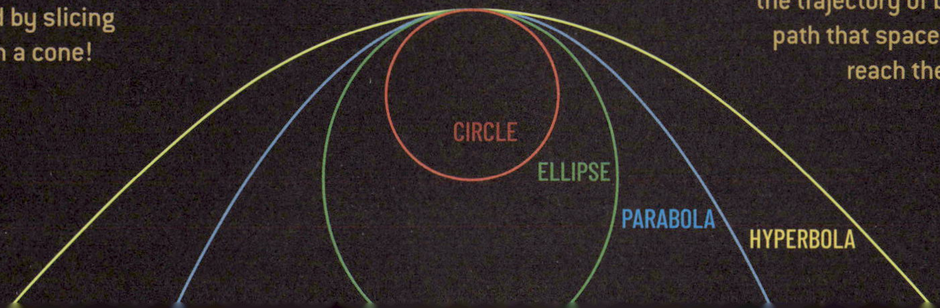

CIRCLE
ELLIPSE
PARABOLA
HYPERBOLA

ROCKET BOOSTER: used to reach Earth's orbit

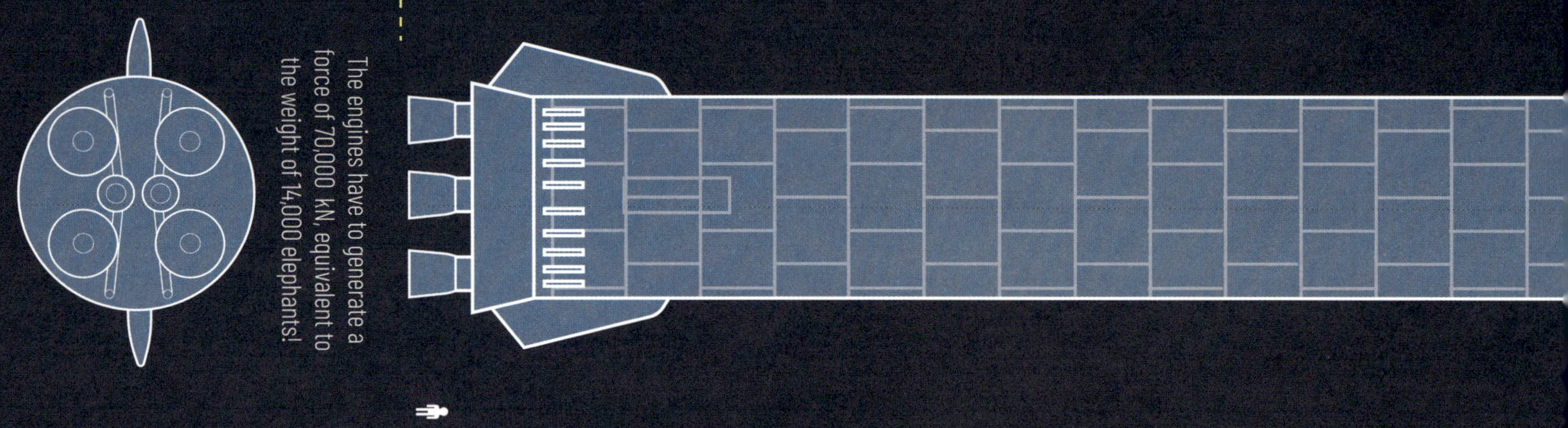

The engines have to generate a force of 70,000 kN, equivalent to the weight of 14,000 elephants!

ENGINES AND FUEL TANK FOR THE ROCKET

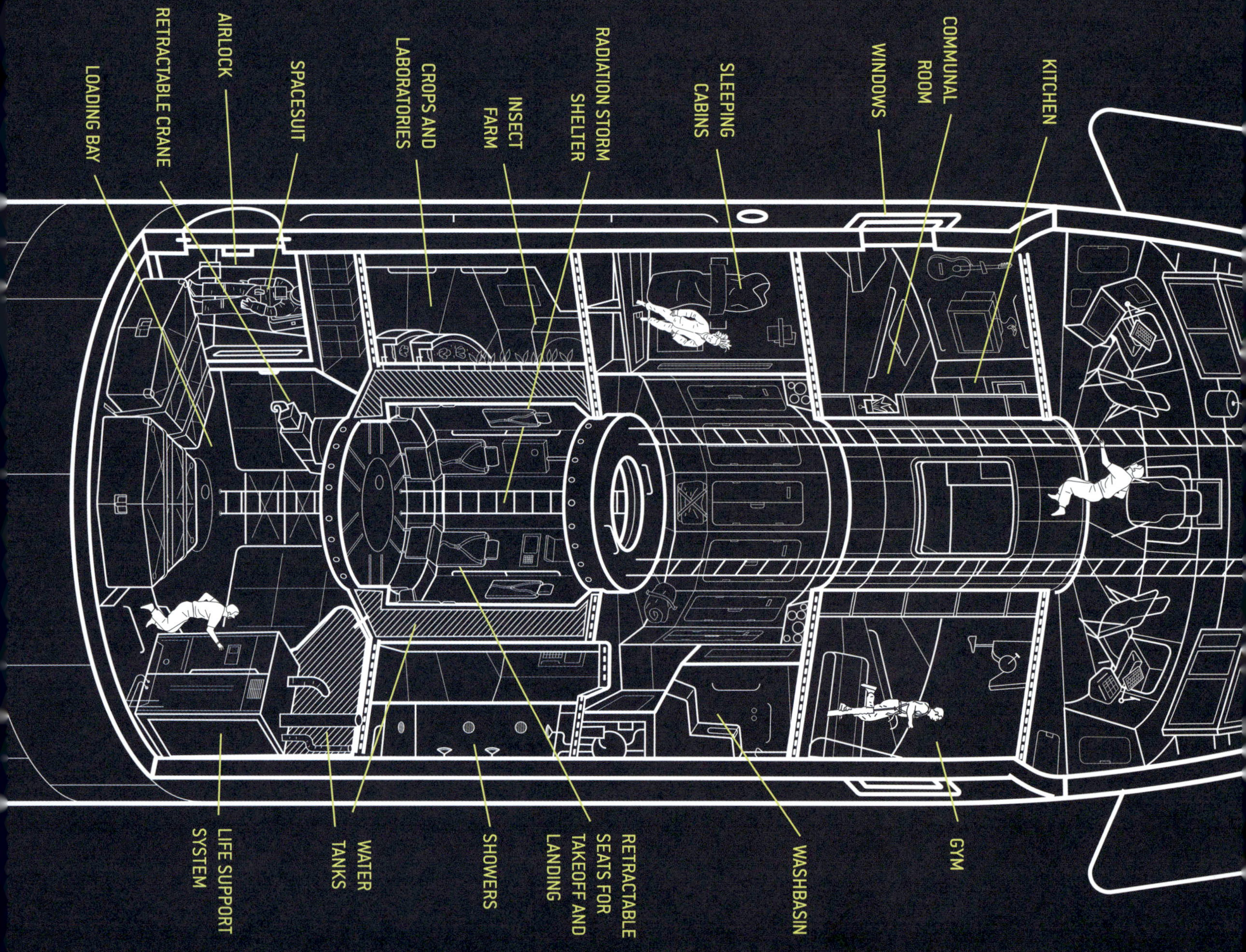

LOADING BAY
RETRACTABLE CRANE
AIRLOCK
SPACESUIT
CROPS AND LABORATORIES
INSECT FARM
RADIATION STORM SHELTER
SLEEPING CABINS
WINDOWS
COMMUNAL ROOM
KITCHEN

LIFE SUPPORT SYSTEM
WATER TANKS
SHOWERS
RETRACTABLE SEATS FOR TAKEOFF AND LANDING
WASHBASIN
GYM

THE SPACECRAFT

CREW QUARTERS

ENGINES AND FUEL TANK FOR THE SPACECRAFT

THE LAUNCH

Several rockets are launched into Earth's orbit.

One spacecraft carries the crew. The others only carry fuel.

The crewed spacecraft begins the journey to Mars.

The crewed spacecraft lands.

Fuel is loaded onto the crewed spacecraft.

On Mars, the spacecraft is loaded with fuel for its return to Earth.

The rocket boosters return to Earth to be reused.

The supply craft return to Earth.

The more weight that is launched, the more fuel the rocket will need to escape Earth's gravity. This is why several launches are planned, with spacecraft taking into Earth's orbit the fuel needed for the journey to Mars.

THE INTERIOR

(CREW QUARTERS)

Playing with gravity

Traveling from the surface of one planet to another requires a series of maneuvers that include takeoff, landing, changes of speed and tilt in orbit, and a long cruise unpropelled by engines. It is an elegant dance between the spacecraft and the forces of gravity.

1. **Launch:** Moving away from Earth's surface requires a powerful rocket capable of overcoming gravity and accelerating in the atmosphere until the spacecraft is orbiting about 125 miles (200 km) above Earth.

2. **Escaping Earth's gravity:** The spacecraft moves away from Earth until it exits Earth's sphere of influence, breaks free from its gravity, and enters the gravitational influence of the Sun.

3. **Orbit around the Sun:** The spacecraft continues its elliptical trajectory around the Sun. This stage is not propelled by the spacecraft's engines, except for a few small corrections to the orbit from time to time.

4. **Entering Mars's gravity:** When the spacecraft has come close enough to Mars to enter its sphere of influence, the planet's gravitational effect gets stronger and it "captures" the spacecraft.

5. **Entry, descent, and landing:** The last stage of the journey ends with the spacecraft landing on the surface of Mars. This stage is referred to as "the seven minutes of terror."

It takes more than four minutes for a radio signal to go from Mars to Earth, and four minutes for it to come back again. This is why spacecraft need to be self-sufficient when it comes to correcting their entry positions, especially during the landing process.

The human factor

A voyage to Mars can take up to ten months. One very important thing to consider about the first crewed missions will be the psychological impact on the astronauts after so much time shut inside. This is why the spacecraft has to be equipped with systems that support the passengers' well-being. These include lighting adapted to Earth's day-night cycles, leisure and social areas, private spaces, and communications systems to talk to family and friends on Earth.

Mission architecture

The more complex a space mission, the more alternative plans have to be considered. For crewed journeys to Mars, there are three basic architectures:

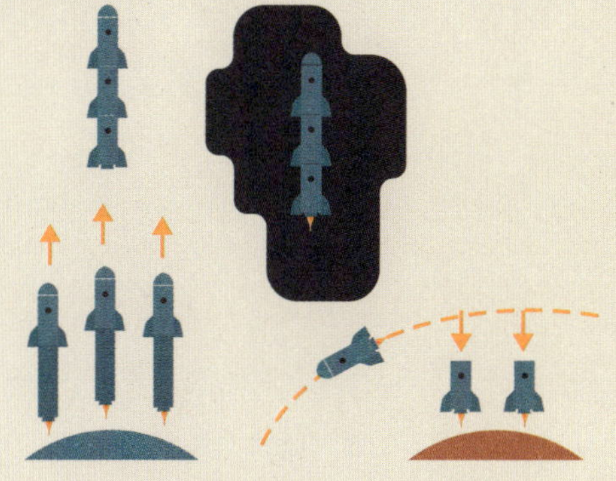

Direct ascent: A single launch of one large spacecraft, capable of traveling and landing without separating into modules. Achieving a launch like this requires designing an extremely powerful rocket. This is the architecture that SpaceX's Starship spacecraft use.

Separation in Mars's orbit: A single launch of a small spacecraft that travels to Mars and separates into modules on arrival. One of the modules descends to the surface, while the others continue orbiting. This keeps the descent module as small as possible and saves fuel. This was the architecture used for the Apollo missions to the Moon.

Assembly in Earth's orbit: The spacecraft is launched in sections using several rockets and is assembled in Earth's orbit. This makes it possible to build a very large spacecraft that could not be launched with a single rocket. Once assembled, it sets off to Mars.

SEVEN MINUTES OF TERROR!

These are the final minutes, and they are very tense. The spacecraft reaches Mars's atmosphere traveling at 12,100 mph (19,500 km/h) and has to brake suddenly for a successful landing.

When the spacecraft comes into contact with the atmosphere, its speed reduces, but the craft needs to be protected from the high temperatures with a heat shield.

Parachutes, airbags, and retrorockets are then used to help the lander reach the ground without any damage.

The spacecraft must perform this whole stage autonomously. Mission control on Earth loses contact with the craft and all they can do is wait for the signal: I AM SAFE ON MARS!

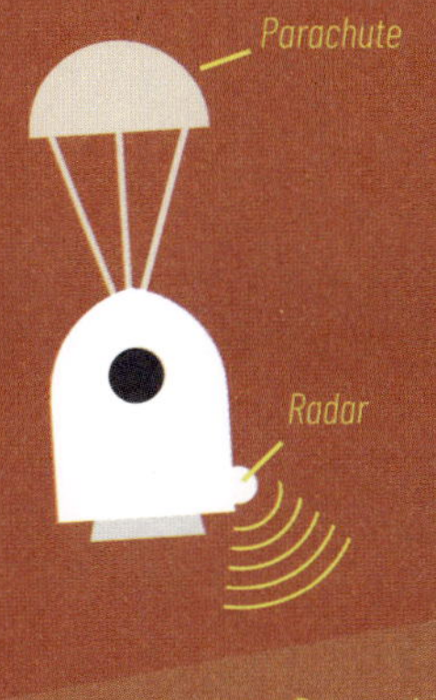

FUTURE VOYAGES

Future spacecraft will be gigantic space stations that will allow us to travel across the solar system fast, comfortably, and carrying huge quantities of cargo and passengers.

ORBITAL SPACECRAFT

Unlike the spacecraft used in the early 21st century, orbital spacecraft won't launch from land or land on a planet's surface. We will be able to build them directly in space and they will be much cheaper, larger, and more efficient.

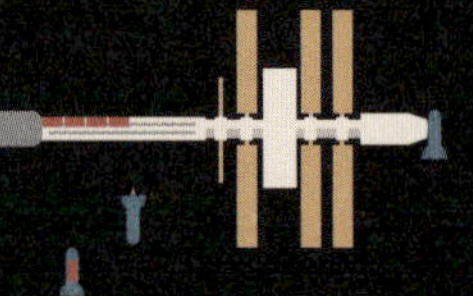

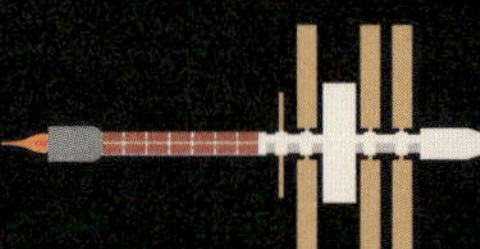

Shuttles will be used to transport cargo and passengers from a planet's surface to the orbital spacecraft.

Artificial gravity

We can use centrifugal force to create artificial gravity. Centrifugal force will be generated by a rotating ring-shaped cabin, which pushes passengers outward. Artificial gravity reduces the physical problems caused by months of weightlessness during the journey.

Centrifugal force is what you feel when you go round a bend in a car or what causes socks to stick to the washing machine drum.

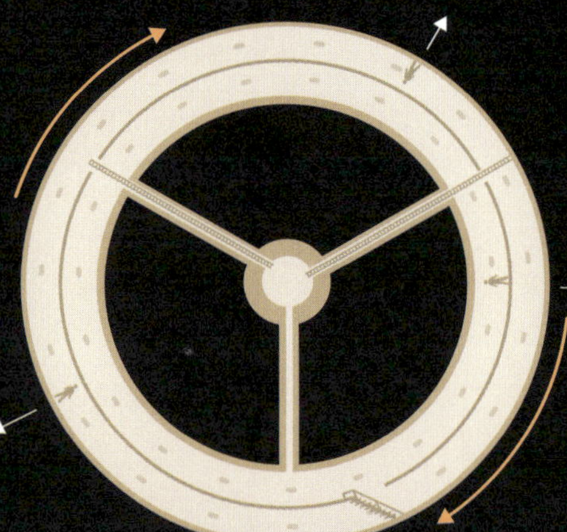

On a journey to Mars, artificial gravity can be gradually reduced, so that the human body can slowly adapt to Martian gravity.

Propulsion system

Loading bay

Shuttle

Photovoltaic (solar) panels

Rotating ring (living space)

Access hatches

Emergency craft

Life support system

Biological systems made up of plants and algae will generate oxygen (O_2) and food and remove carbon dioxide (CO_2). The system partly copies the environment we have on Earth. It provides fresh food and saves weight on long journeys.

Artificial intelligence

Artificial intelligence (AI) will manage most of the important processes, such as piloting the spacecraft, monitoring the spacecraft's systems, and producing food and oxygen.

PROPULSION SYSTEMS

HOW LIKELY IS THIS? / JOURNEY TIME

System in use — 7–9 months

Chemical propulsion

The engine propels the craft by expelling gases at high speed through a duct. The gases are accelerated by burning fuel to convert chemical energy into motion.

System developed — 5–6 months

Ion thrusters

The spacecraft is propelled by a jet of ions accelerated by large electric fields. These ion thrusters work side-by-side with the chemical propulsion engines to reduce the journey time to Mars.

Under development

Fission engines

These detonate mini-nuclear bombs that propel the spacecraft with their shockwave.

15 days

Solar sails

An extremely powerful laser propels the spacecraft using a sail. The main problem with this system is the huge amount of power needed to fuel the lasers.

1 day

Fusion engines

Hydrogen present in our space neighborhood (space is NOT empty—there are 125 hydrogen atoms in a quart or liter of space) is collected and used to power a nuclear fusion reactor.

Almost science fiction — 1 hour

Antimatter engines

Propulsion is achieved by the annihilation between matter and anti-matter. The collision between a particle and its corresponding anti-particle releases a huge amount of energy, with 100% efficiency. A few grams would be enough to travel much further in space than Mars!

Science fiction — < 5 minutes

Curvature engine *(Warp Drive)*

This engine would make it possible to travel much faster than light, thanks to the distortion of the space-time fabric produced by "exotic" matter, which propels the spacecraft like a surfer on a wave.

SETTING UP BASE ZERO

To make sure a settlement on Mars survives, we will first need to establish a base settlement. From here, we could deploy the essential infrastructures and make sure that all vital systems function properly under the harsh Martian conditions before any settlers arrive. Several cargo missions would be needed to deploy all the technology, machinery, and tools needed.

1: Arrival (and return) vehicle

The spacecraft lands with all the modules packed inside. It has an unloading system (a crane) and some autonomous energy.

It can load supplies from the base for a return journey or act as a shuttle to take equipment up and down. It uses a combination of basic gases and oxygen (O_2) as fuel.

Needs: *Liquefied gases.*
Provides: *This vehicle could house some of the modules for the initial base (living space, workshops, laboratories).*

2: Resource collectors

For obtaining the necessary resources from Mars's atmosphere and soil.

The basic resources are carbon dioxide (CO_2) and water (H_2O). We can collect carbon dioxide from Mars's atmosphere, using compressors and filters to remove dust particles, and extract water from the soil by heating hydrated clays to around 750°F (400°C). The ideal site for the water extraction module is an area with loose regolith (sand and stones) so that a mechanized rover can transport the clay.

Needs: *Energy, clay.*
Provides: *Compressed Martian atmosphere and water vapor.*

3: Chemical plant

For transforming simple resources into more complex substances.

When water and carbon dioxide are processed we get simple atoms or molecules, some as important as carbon (C), hydrogen (H_2), and oxygen. These can either be used directly (for example, oxygen for breathing) or as ingredients in the organic chemicals on which life on Earth and our technology are based.

Needs: *Water and compressed Martian atmosphere, energy.*
Provides: *Carbon and basic essential gases.*

4: Tanks

For storing essential gases and the resources collected (carbon dioxide and water).

Tanks are used to store pressurized or liquefied gases at a very low temperature. The tanks have to be very robust to withstand the extreme temperatures on Mars. Storing gases means storing energy. For example, hydrogen with oxygen can be used to generate electricity, or combusting gases with oxygen can be used as fuel.

Needs: *Gas and liquid resources, energy.*
Provides: *Distribution of resources and energy.*

9: Energy modules

For generating the electrical and thermal energy needed for the base to function.

The most practical starting point is a few small nuclear reactors, as they generate power continuously (between 30 and 100 kW each). Solar panels provide extra power and are a backup system in case of failure. For safety reasons, the nuclear modules are located a distance away from the base.

Needs: *Maintenance.*
Provides: *Energy.*

8: Housing

For the first settlers and builders of the city.

At first, people live in modules on the planet's surface or inside the spacecraft. This housing has water recycling systems, a life support system, climate control, etc., and provides the minimum comfort needed for the physical and mental health of the people who live there. The structures are covered with regolith from Mars, which reduces the impact of radiation and extreme temperatures.

Needs: *Gases, energy, life support.*
Provides: *The essentials for the settlers' immediate survival, including basic services.*

7: Greenhouses

For transforming carbon dioxide and water into food, fibers, or even medicines.

All the basic nutrients needed for the survival of the city's inhabitants are grown in greenhouses, using highly efficient crops and bioreactors (such as fungi and bacteria). The system should use and reuse all materials to the full and avoid the need for imports and resource extraction, etc.

Needs: *Gases, water, organic waste, trace elements, energy.*
Provides: *Food and advanced materials.*

5: Surface vehicles

For journeys, transporting materials, and building infrastructure.

The minimum requirements are: one rover to transport crew members, another to move and tow large parts, and a third one for excavation (digging). Of the three, at least one needs to have a pressurized cabin. The vehicles require a workshop module for maintenance and repairs. Also, the rovers and the machinery have to function remotely or self-sufficiently to minimize human activity on the surface.

Needs: *Energy (or fuel), a repairs workshop.*
Provides: *Transport and deployment of base modules. Excavation and earth moving.*

6: Workshops and laboratories

For complex tasks: making components, repairs, and chemical processes for advanced products.

The workshop is equipped with flexible and robust technology that is easy to repair using simple by-products of the stored gases. At least one laboratory module is needed for scientific experiments and maintenance tasks on the base.

Needs: *Gases, energy, temperature control, life support.*
Provides: *Infrastructure maintenance, advanced products, basic research.*

Mars's first inhabitants will be scientists, architects, engineers, and other workers who will establish the bases to create the first city. But building structures in a hostile environment like Mars involves a very different set of challenges from those faced by architects and engineers on Earth. These challenges will shape the way we build and live on the Red Planet.

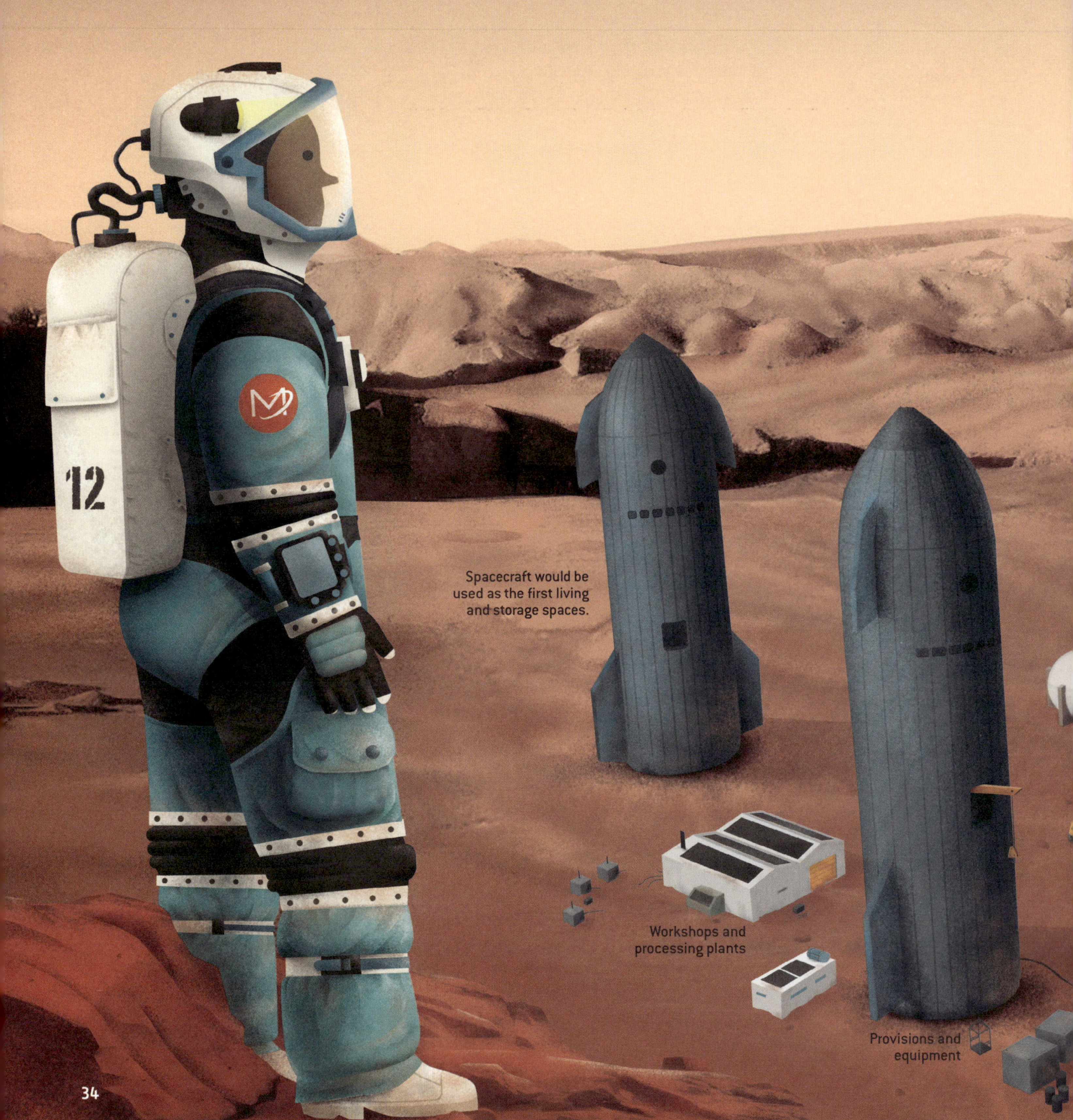

THE CHALLENGES OF BUILDING ON MARS

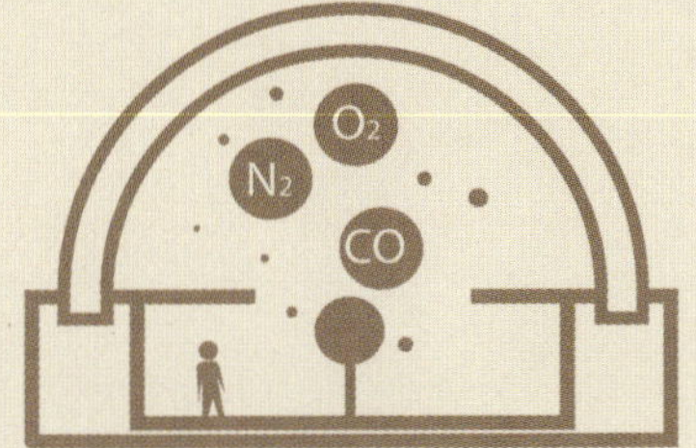

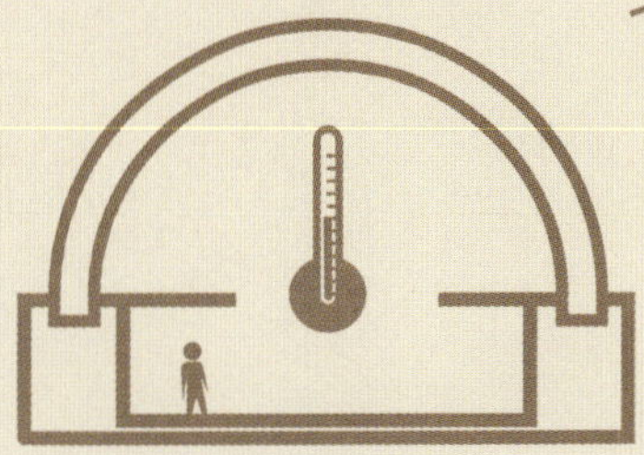

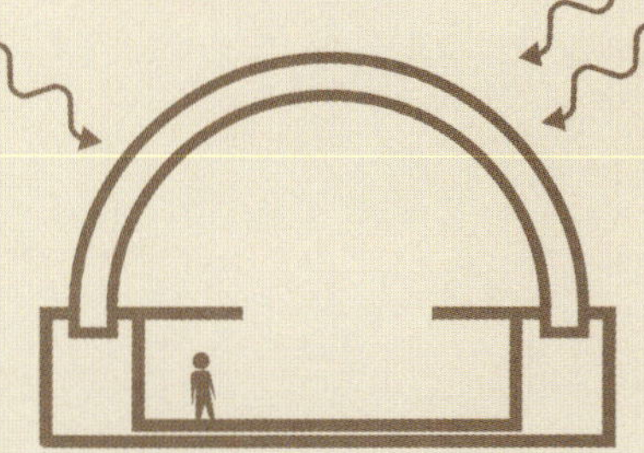

PRESSURIZATION

The atmospheric pressure on Mars is so low that we cannot survive in it for more than a few seconds. If we want to create livable spaces on Mars, we need to recreate Earth's atmospheric pressure. Building livable spaces is a big challenge, because pressurization involves a huge amount of outward pressure.

To prevent buildings from exploding, they need to be solid structures made from tough materials that are easy to obtain and process on Mars. The design of these structures should not be psychologically suffocating.

(👁 pp. 14–15)

ATMOSPHERE

We need to live in an atmosphere that is chemically similar to Earth's. Recreating this on Mars requires a constant supply of oxygen. We also need to control the content of water vapor and other gases such as carbon dioxide (CO_2), as well as the products of reactions related to biological and human activity, such as methane (CH_4), ammonia (NH_3), nitrogen oxide, etc.

Technology or biological systems could be used to filter the air in closed ecosystems that mimic processes found on Earth.

(👁 pp. 14–15)

TEMPERATURE

The materials used for building need to maintain a comfortable temperature inside and cope with the extreme temperature differences outside. The contrast between day and night on Mars can be more than 212°F (100°C), and even during the day there can be major differences between sun and shade.

The materials need to thermally insulate the inside from the outside, while keeping their mechanical properties.

(👁 pp. 16–17)

RADIATION

Radiation causes serious health problems within months. The most dangerous source of radiation is the high-energy particles of cosmic rays.

Looking horizontally through glass is not very dangerous, but the roofs of buildings will need to be protected. A couple of yards of regolith (sand and stones) or a few dozen inches of materials rich in hydrogen atoms (such as water or plastics) may be enough.

(👁 pp. 12–13)

One way to reduce the environmental hazards on Mars is to **construct buildings underground**. This does not completely remove all the dangers, but the Martian rock and regolith (sand and stones) around and above the structures absorbs the pressure from inside the buildings, helps control the temperature, and provides protection from radiation. At the same time, it uses Martian soil, an on-site resource.

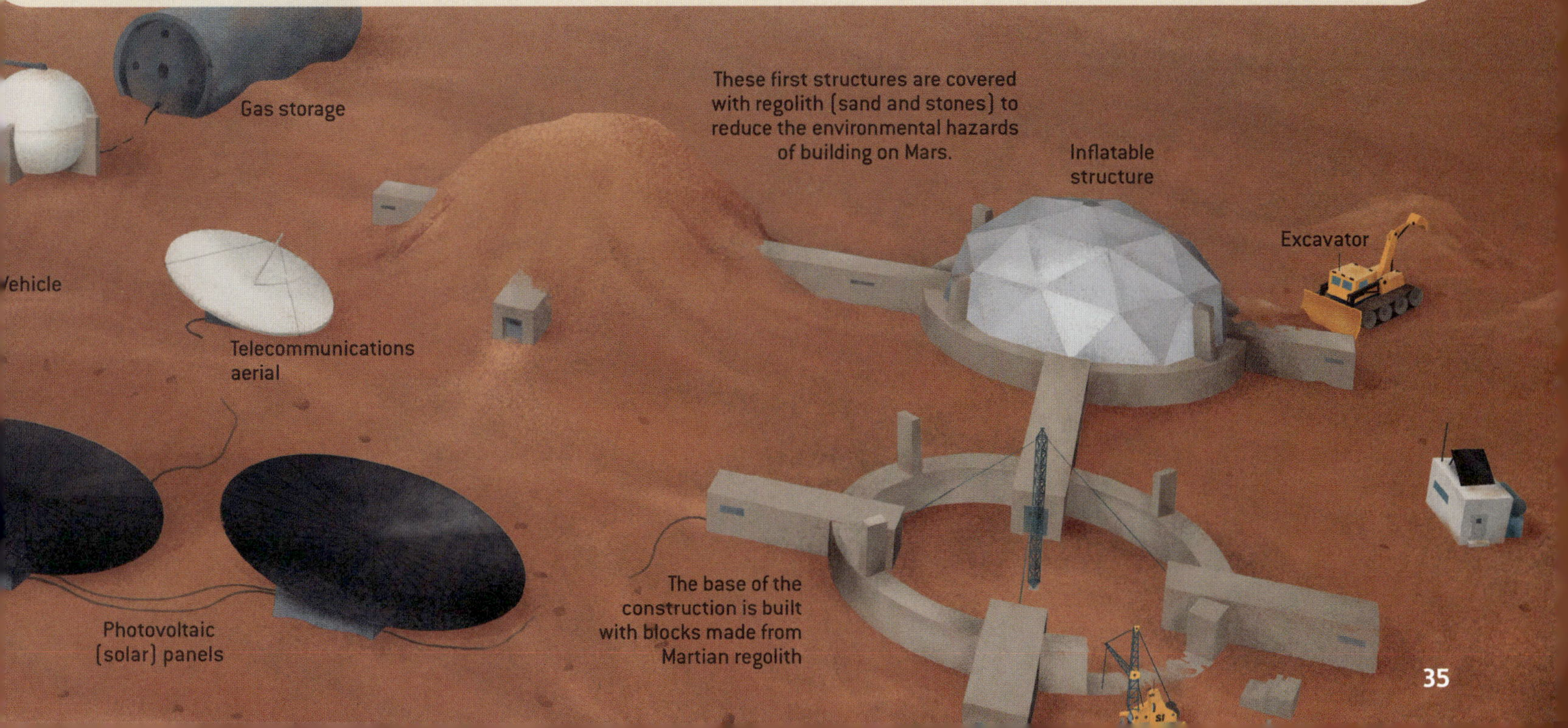

Gas storage

These first structures are covered with regolith (sand and stones) to reduce the environmental hazards of building on Mars.

Inflatable structure

Excavator

Vehicle

Telecommunications aerial

Photovoltaic (solar) panels

The base of the construction is built with blocks made from Martian regolith

A city on Mars

Building a city underground reduces the most immediate environmental risks on Mars. A vertical city makes the best use of space, and is almost totally protected from the elements. The city is built into a cliff and gives people who live there access to all areas. Living spaces are spread over a network of tunnels, and other areas provide natural light and views outside. Energy is produced on the plateau at the top of the cliff, and big communal areas are in the valley below.

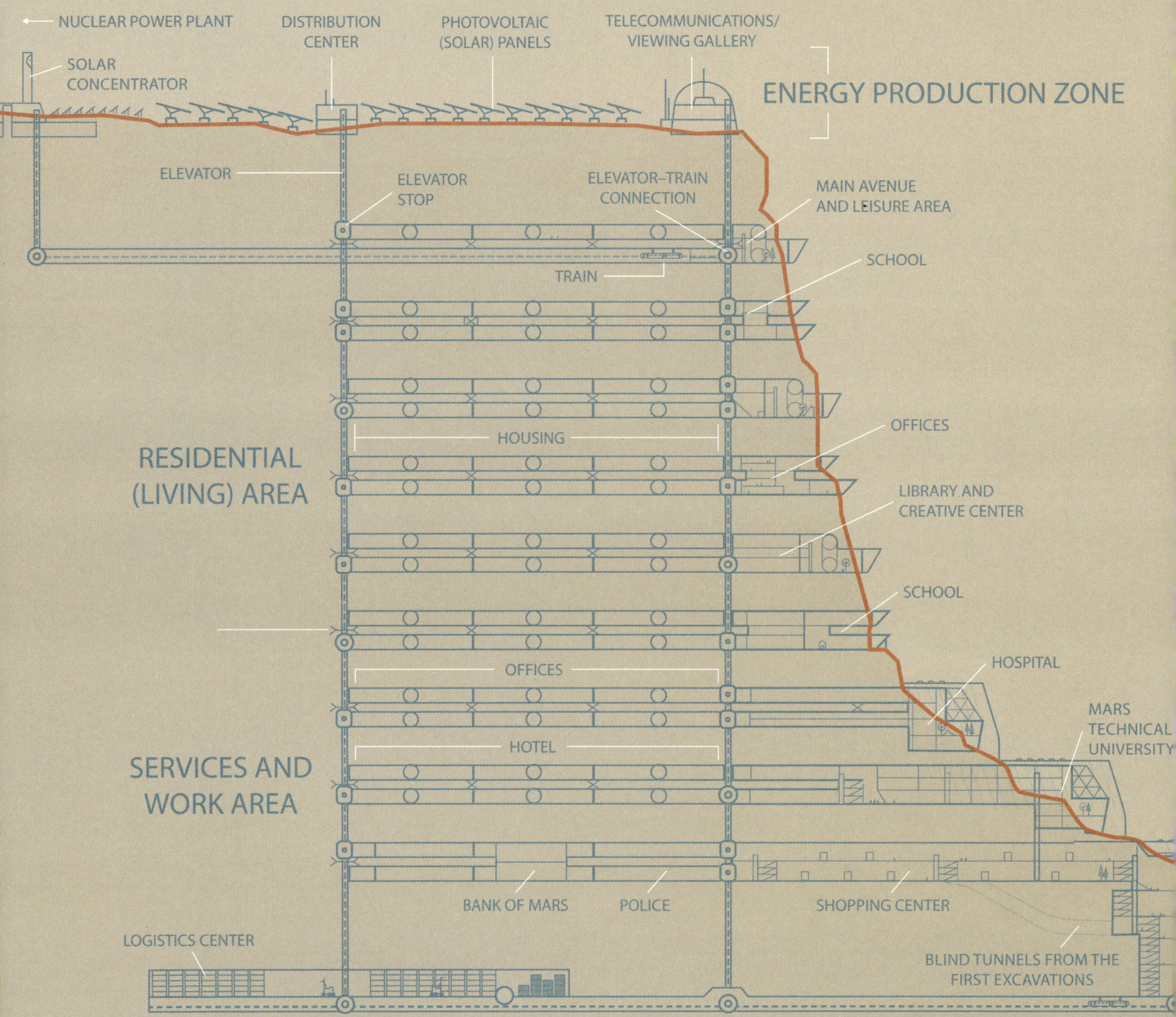

But a city is much more than housing and buildings. It must provide comfort, space, and connections for the people who live there, and be a place where life, culture, and the economy can grow and develop naturally. This city concept is based on a system of large interconnected tunnels that branch off into cylinders containing spaces for different purposes. Individual cylinders serve as buildings, and groups of cylinders as districts.

RESIDENTIAL DISTRICTS
As well as private spaces such as housing, the city needs to provide services and communal (shared) areas such as schools, parks, shops, cafes, and spaces where people can socialize.

WORK SPACES
There will be offices, workshops, and work districts for the city's services and for new businesses, so that the Martian economy and culture can develop.

PUBLIC SPACES AND GOVERNMENT
As well as the government and administrative headquarters, the city will provide all the public spaces that are needed, such as sports stadiums, museums, hotels, etc.

PUBLIC TRANSPORT
The city will provide a rapid transport system, combining vertical elevators with trains that cover the length and breadth of the city and provide a spaceport link.

INDUSTRIAL AND CULTIVATION ZONE
The city will need to be self-sufficient. It will manufacture and produce almost everything it needs, and have storage and goods distribution systems.

ENERGY PRODUCTION
There will be a variety of energy production and distribution systems to safely maintain life support systems throughout the city.

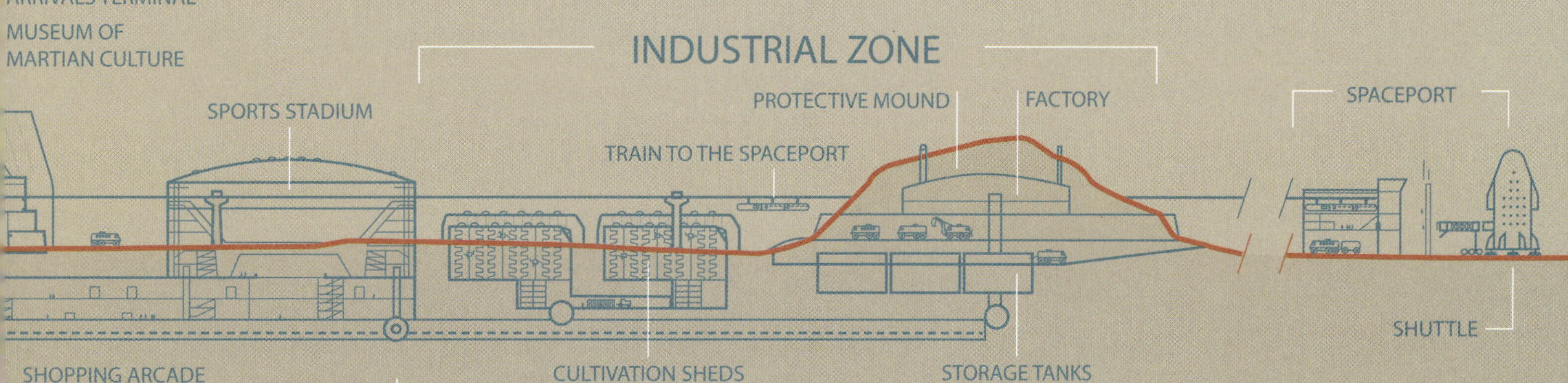

HOUSING

AND RESIDENTIAL AREAS

Inhabitants of Mars will need private spaces to live in. But homes on Mars will be limited in size and have no windows or access to the outside, as they will be located inside a series of interconnected tunnels as part of a complex city.

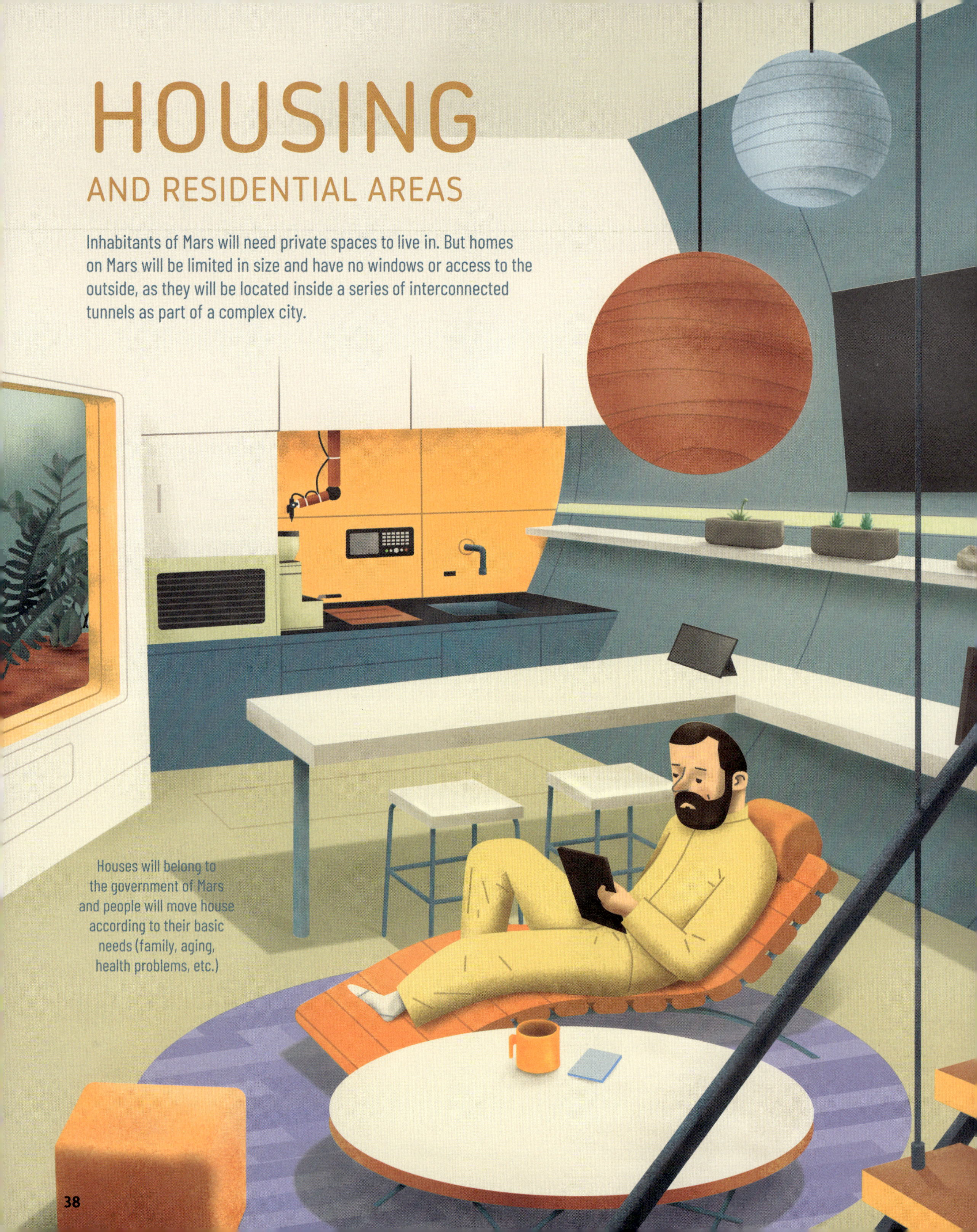

Houses will belong to the government of Mars and people will move house according to their basic needs (family, aging, health problems, etc.)

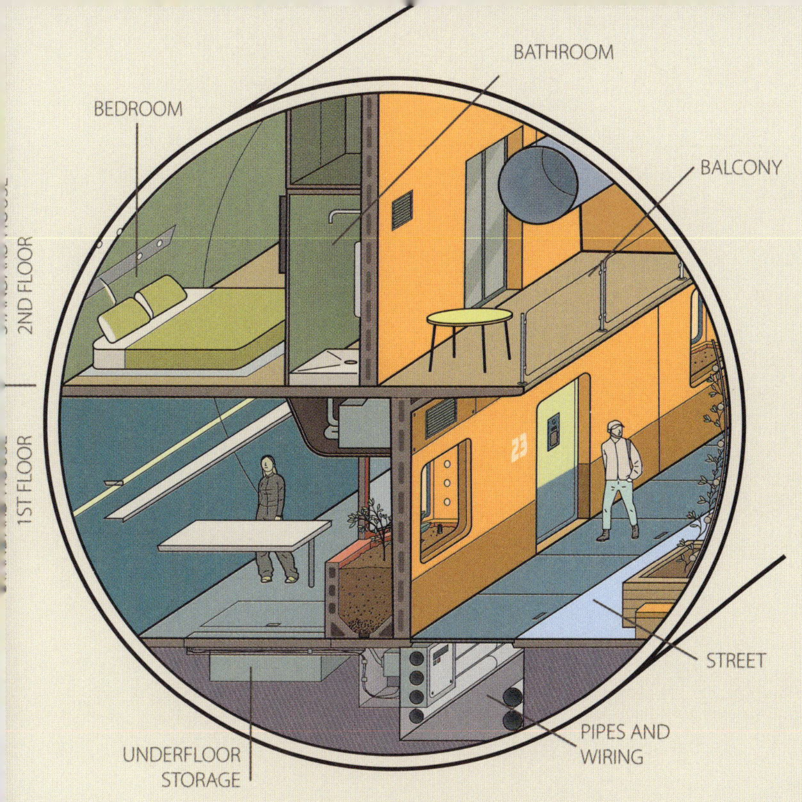

BATHROOM
BEDROOM
BALCONY
2ND FLOOR
1ST FLOOR
STREET
UNDERFLOOR STORAGE
PIPES AND WIRING

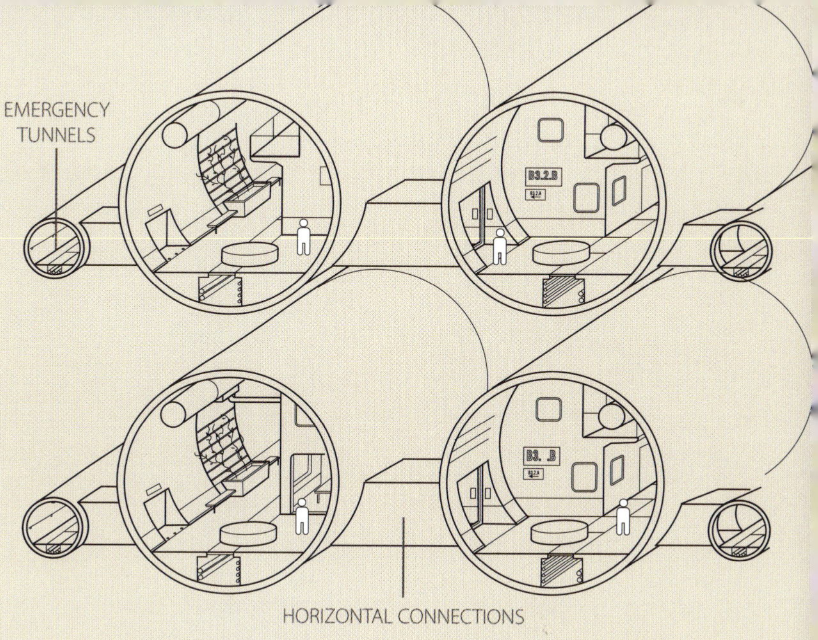

EMERGENCY TUNNELS
HORIZONTAL CONNECTIONS

CROSS SECTION OF A RESIDENTIAL BLOCK

HORIZONTAL BUILDINGS

Individual living spaces will form housing modules, and there will also be streets, public spaces, and local services such as launderettes and clinics. The housing modules will be grouped in sets of four interconnected tunnels, which penetrate hundreds of yards into the rock, forming a horizontal block. The area for services, leisure activities, and community life is located on the cliff face.

VIEW OF AN APARTMENT BLOCK FROM ABOVE

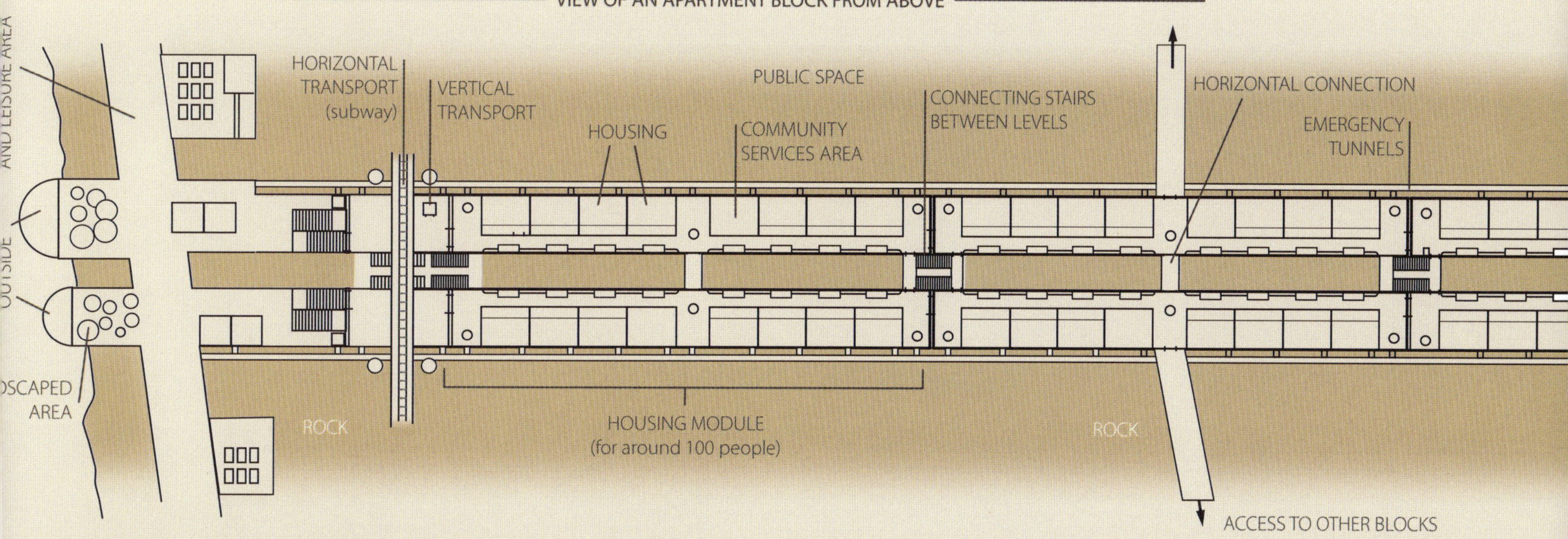

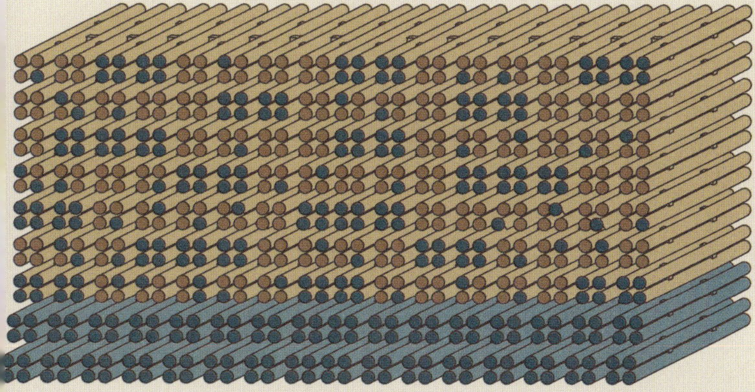

THE DISTRICT

A certain number of blocks will form a district. The upper levels of the district are mostly housing modules, while large spaces such as universities, logistics centers, and hospitals are located on the lower levels. The service areas and workplaces are mainly found in the communal areas on the cliff face, with views to the outside.

THE COST PER CITIZEN

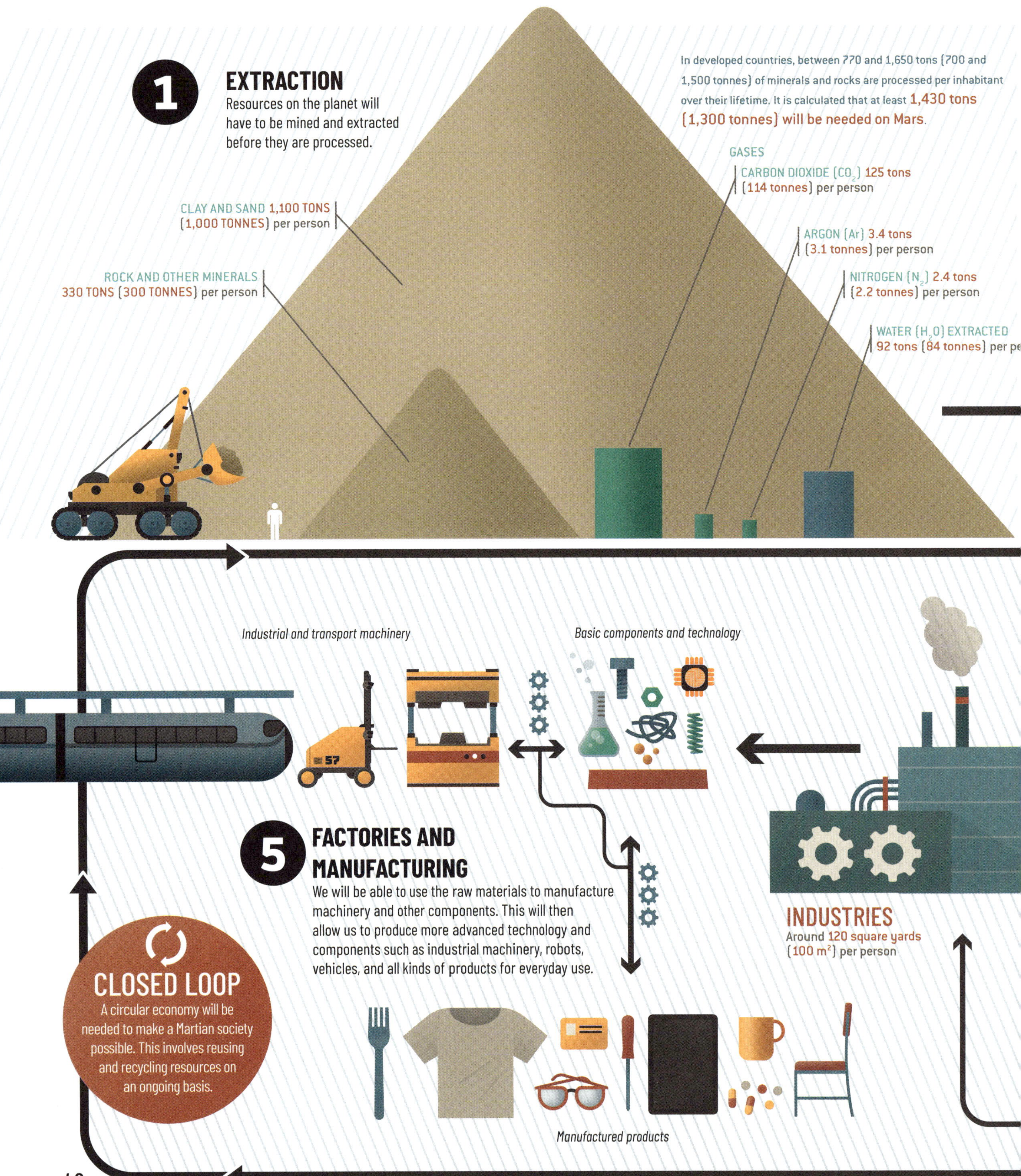

Setting up a society needs resources and infrastructure. On Earth, we use (and sometimes use up) our planet's resources. Creating and maintaining a city on Mars poses enormous technological challenges. A lot of different processes are needed to build spaces, produce energy, and maintain life support systems. All this costs a lot in resources for each inhabitant.

HUGE QUANTITIES OF ENERGY ARE NEEDED TO CARRY OUT ALL THESE PROCESSES.

2 TRANSFORMATION

The resources extracted on Mars will be processed into basic materials (such as metals, liquids, and gases) using industrial processes that require a lot of energy.

RAW MATERIALS

GRAVEL AND CEMENT
343 tons (311 tonnes) per person

IRON AND STEEL
66 tons (60 tonnes) per person

POLYMERS
40 tons (36 tonnes) per person

ADVANCED MATERIALS
9.9 tons (8.9 tonnes) per person

SIMPLE BY-PRODUCTS
40 tons (36 tonnes) per person

SPECIAL METALS
8.6 tons (7.8 tonnes) per person

4 BUILDING INFRASTRUCTURE

This infrastructure is needed to support the city's operations: energy, communications, living spaces, food production, transport networks, etc.

3

AI

Artificial intelligence (AI) will help us to manage the complicated system and make sure it works without relying so much on humans.

LIFE SUPPORT SYSTEMS

Responsible for maintaining a livable environment

WATER: 88 tons (80 tonnes) per person
CARBON DIOXIDE: 125 tons (114 tonnes) per person

HOUSING, SERVICES, AND COMMUNAL SPACES

300 square yards (250 m²) per person

GREENHOUSES AND FARMS

Around 120 square yards (100 m²) per person

Each inhabitant requires between 50 kW and 120 kW of power.
(in developed countries on Earth, each person uses around 10 kW.)

ENERGY INFRASTRUCTURES

Solar concentrator 330 square yards (276 m²) per person
Photovoltaic 1,650 square yards (1,380 m²) per person
Nuclear 330 square yards (276 m²) per person

STORAGE TANKS

7,130 gallons (27 m³) per person

COMMUNICATIONS NETWORKS

TRANSPORT NETWORKS

Within and out of the city, and between planets

COMMUNITY LIFE

On Mars, practically all human activity will take place underground. Therefore, it is very important that the city has large, well-lit, and well-protected spaces where people can gather and socialize. The large areas used for sport and culture will be located in the city's lower levels, with spacious half-buried (not excavated) buildings.

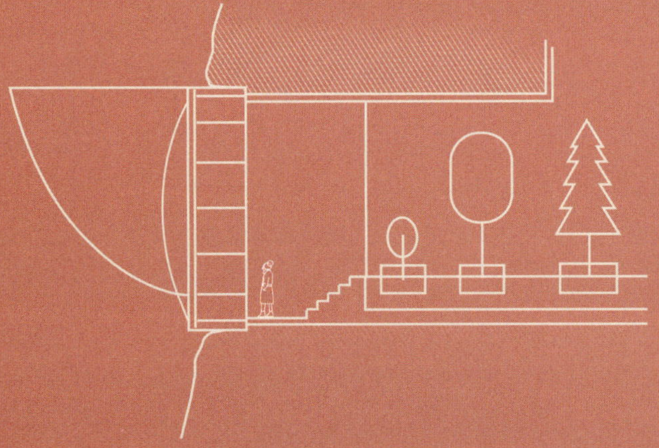

OPENINGS

Housing blocks and districts will have small communal spaces, but the main communal areas will be in the valley and particularly in the "openings" zone. Here, there are huge windows that look out onto the outside world, letting natural light in and giving people views of the landscape.

The double-height tunnel is achieved by joining two tunnels together.

Leisure areas and shopping arcades will be located in these naturally lit spaces inside spacious, double-height tunnels. Services such as hospitals, gyms, schools, and offices are also located here.

12B-32B
ARES
NEWS
12A-32A
MRT
MRT

ENERGY

Humans have evolved to live on Earth. We are adapted to its atmospheric pressure (which also provides us with the oxygen we breathe) and to its gravity. We have plenty of liquid water, the temperature is pleasant, and, to top it all, the planet provides us with food.

On Mars, things are much more hostile: its atmosphere is very thin and there is practically no oxygen, there is no ozone layer to block ultraviolet radiation, temperatures are extremely low, gravity is three times less than on Earth, and, to top it all, there is nothing edible.

But with today's technology and enough energy, we can turn Mars into a planet where humans can live.

We will need energy to carry out all the technological, chemical, and industrial processes that are essential to transform the environment and develop a Martian society and economy.

NUCLEAR ENERGY

The advantage of nuclear reactors is that they generate a lot of energy with only a small amount of fuel. They would be a good first option on Mars, because nuclear fuel can be transported from Earth. We would need a few grams per inhabitant.

However, the infrastructure needed to operate a nuclear reactor safely requires a huge amount of materials (concrete and metals). These materials can be sourced on-site in Mars.

One day in the future, our Martian city could use thorium reactors, as thorium is an element that we know exists in reasonably large quantities on the surface of Mars. Thorium reactors (which are under development at the moment) should be safer than uranium reactors too.

At least 30% of our energy should not depend on the Sun.

SOLAR CONCENTRATORS

Solar concentrators use mirrors to focus the Sun's light on a point to heat water. This produces steam that is used to turn a turbine and generate electricity.

The disadvantage of solar concentrators is that they are affected by the darkening of Mars's atmosphere during dust storms. However, their components can be produced from relatively simple local materials (iron, glass, wiring, and pipes), making them easier to build than photovoltaic (solar) panels.

STORAGE

We have to take into account that there is no sunlight at night and our life support system must never run out of energy. So we will have to use different kinds of storage systems (such as synthetic fuels and chemical batteries) to store energy.

One of the big challenges we face is making the components used to produce energy. For example, to make a solar panel we will need to collect and process materials for manufacturing. All this requires energy that is not immediately available. Therefore, things will have to be done gradually and in stages.

PHOTOVOLTAIC (SOLAR) PANELS

Solar panels harness sunlight to generate electricity directly. On missions to Mars, they have already been successfully used to power surface rovers and satellites in orbit. Unlike solar concentrators, solar panels use semiconductors to convert sunlight into energy, which are very difficult to manufacture on Mars.

It is estimated that keeping a human on Mars over the long term requires constant power of around 50 KW, of which 40 KW will be for the greenhouses. If on top of that we want to develop a city of a million inhabitants in less than 50 years, the power required per citizen rises to around 120 KW.

Photovoltaic surface area needed per human: 950 square yards (800 m^2) at the Martian equator, or up to 3,000 square yards (2,500 m^2) near the poles.

Approximately 70% of the energy required will come from the Sun.

*The **Life Support System** would be used mainly for generating oxygen to breathe, creating an environment with a pleasant temperature and pressure, recycling gases and water, and producing food.*

__Electricity__ is vital for lighting, transport, and for running all kinds of communication networks, machinery, and household appliances.

*Factories on Mars will require energy to **manufacture everything needed** for everyday life: elevators, trains, cables, forks, chairs, etc.*

__Food production__ is the process that requires the most energy of all.

__Water__ is a very difficult resource to obtain, so it must be permanently recycled in a closed and self-sustaining loop.

PARKS and green spaces

Mars has no magnetic field and a very thin atmosphere. Because of this, solar and cosmic radiation are too intense on the surface for plants and animals to survive over the long term. So, if we want to enjoy green spaces with outside views, we will need to protect them with structures that block the radiation, but at the same time allow us to look out at the landscape and the cycles of day and night. Green spaces will be located in residential districts and in the lower part of the valley, which is where the large communal areas are. They will feature landscaped public parks, which will give views of the outside world through domes and lookout points.

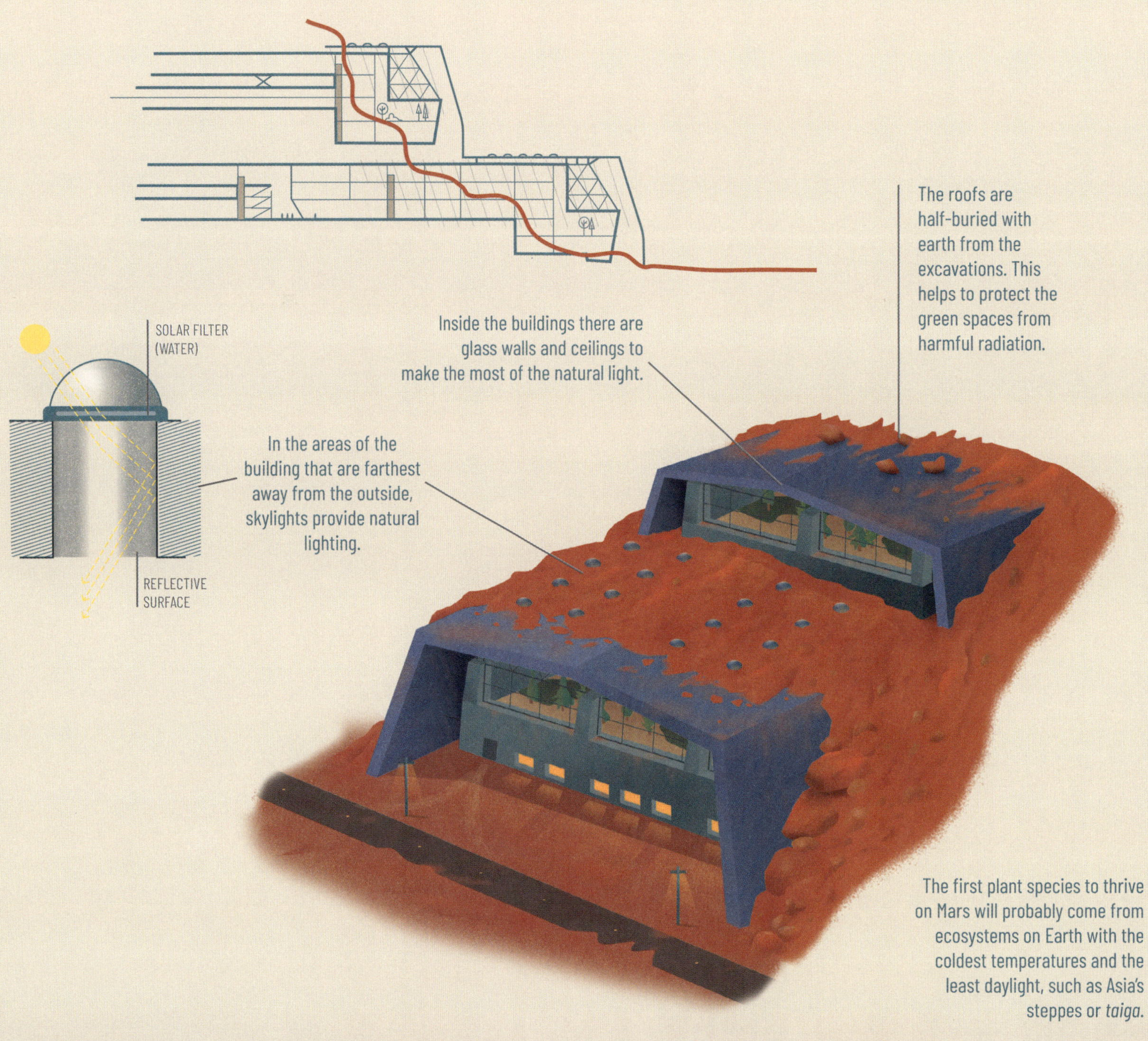

The roofs are half-buried with earth from the excavations. This helps to protect the green spaces from harmful radiation.

Inside the buildings there are glass walls and ceilings to make the most of the natural light.

In the areas of the building that are farthest away from the outside, skylights provide natural lighting.

The first plant species to thrive on Mars will probably come from ecosystems on Earth with the coldest temperatures and the least daylight, such as Asia's steppes or *taiga*.

MARTIAN DIET

Food provides the energy and nutrients that we need to function and grow. It also plays an important part in our physical and mental well-being. The basic Martian diet will have to provide for all our needs and also be produced efficiently and sustainably. Crops and other organism-based systems could be used to produce materials such as fibers (cotton, hemp, wool) and building materials (wood, bamboo, etc.)

FARM ANIMALS

Typical farm animals (such as chickens, pigs, and fish) are not a very efficient source of nutrients. But we will have to include them in our Martian diet (in a very low percentage) because they are high in energy and act as resource stores.

ALGAE

Algae and micro-algae such as spirulina could provide food in the form of salads, cookies, tablets, and drinks. They can also be used as fertilizers and as part of the water filtration process, and they can process carbon dioxide (CO_2) and produce oxygen (O_2) more efficiently than plants.

INSECTS

Insect farming is a much quicker, cheaper, and more efficient way to obtain animal proteins, so it will almost certainly form part of the Martian diet.

SYNTHETIC FOOD

Producing synthetic meat or growing fungi in bioreactors could be part of a diet that, over the long term, could produce new, creative recipes and foods unique to Mars.

A **BIOREACTOR** *is a device that is used to grow cells or microorganisms through biochemical processes.*

AGRICULTURE MODULES *will be important structures in Martian settlements. They will be capable of growing plants in an atmosphere that has a lot of carbon dioxide—like Mars's atmosphere—which will reduce the cost of building and maintaining them. The pressure of the atmosphere, just 25% of Earth's, will not be suitable for humans, so automated machinery will be used.*

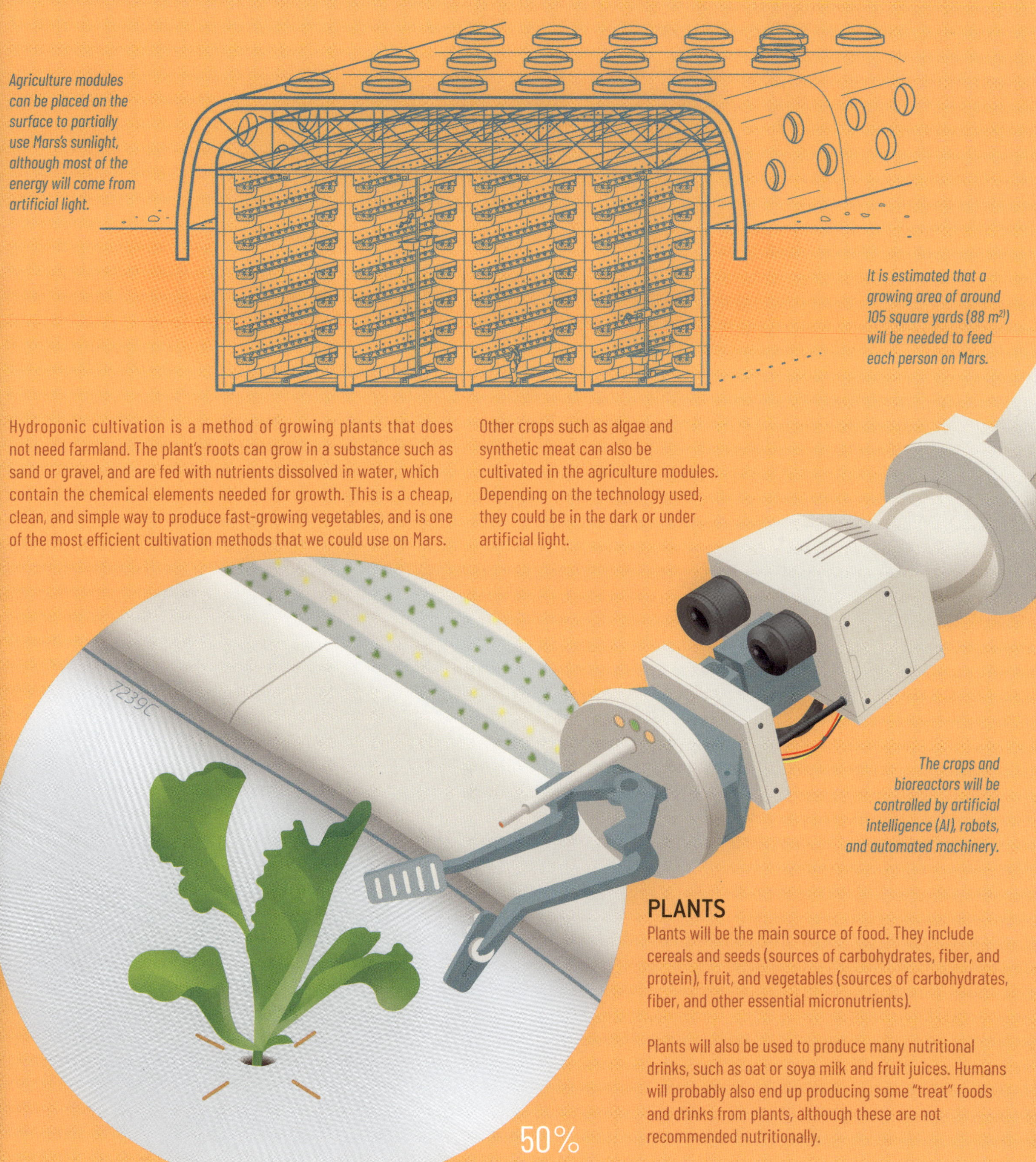

Agriculture modules can be placed on the surface to partially use Mars's sunlight, although most of the energy will come from artificial light.

It is estimated that a growing area of around 105 square yards (88 m²) will be needed to feed each person on Mars.

Hydroponic cultivation is a method of growing plants that does not need farmland. The plant's roots can grow in a substance such as sand or gravel, and are fed with nutrients dissolved in water, which contain the chemical elements needed for growth. This is a cheap, clean, and simple way to produce fast-growing vegetables, and is one of the most efficient cultivation methods that we could use on Mars.

Other crops such as algae and synthetic meat can also be cultivated in the agriculture modules. Depending on the technology used, they could be in the dark or under artificial light.

The crops and bioreactors will be controlled by artificial intelligence (AI), robots, and automated machinery.

PLANTS

Plants will be the main source of food. They include cereals and seeds (sources of carbohydrates, fiber, and protein), fruit, and vegetables (sources of carbohydrates, fiber, and other essential micronutrients).

Plants will also be used to produce many nutritional drinks, such as oat or soya milk and fruit juices. Humans will probably also end up producing some "treat" foods and drinks from plants, although these are not recommended nutritionally.

TRANSPORT

The transport network is designed to allow people to get from one part of the city to another in just a few minutes. There will be two connecting methods of transport: a vertical one (elevators), and a horizontal one (subway lines).

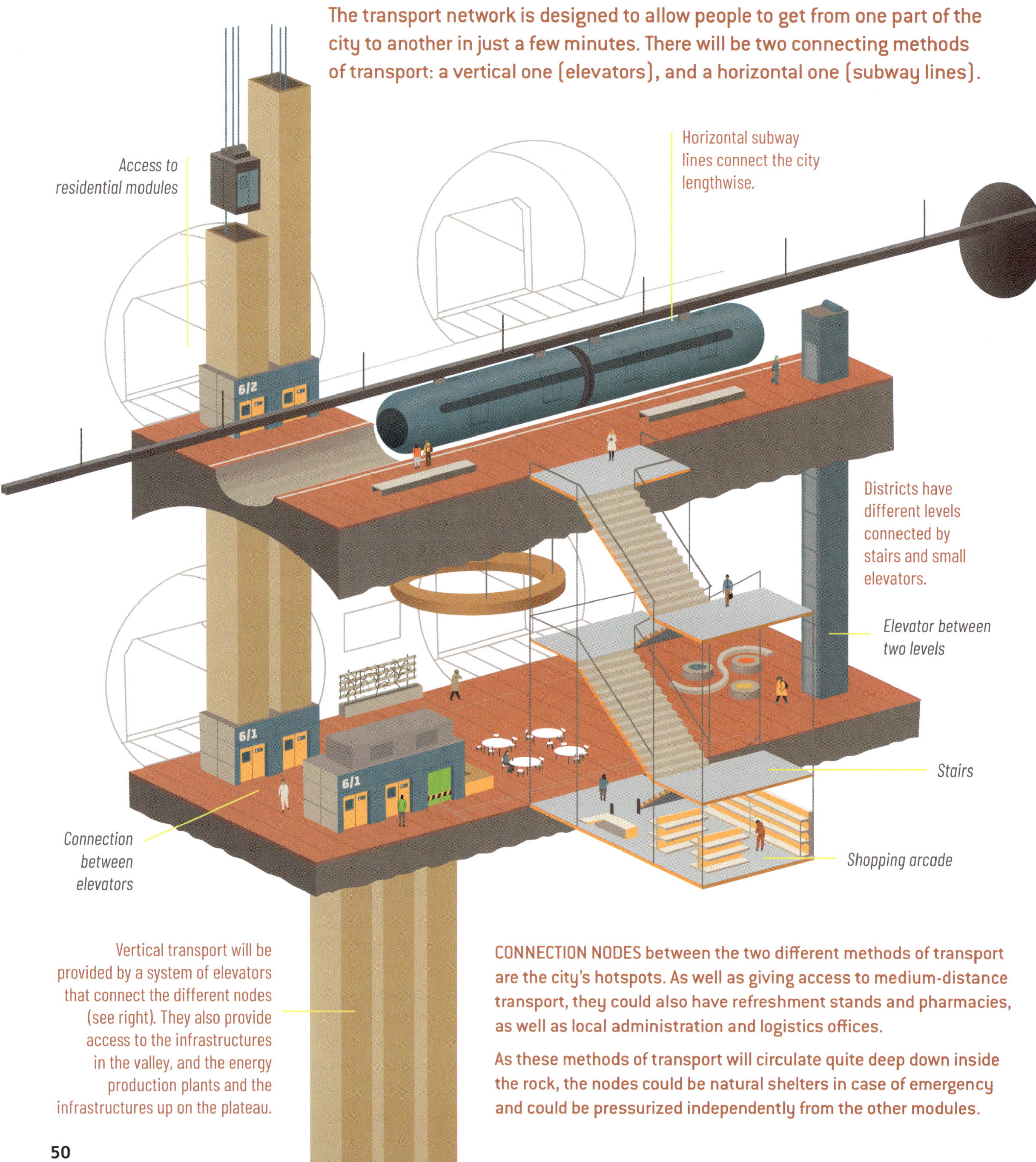

Vertical transport will be provided by a system of elevators that connect the different nodes (see right). They also provide access to the infrastructures in the valley, and the energy production plants and the infrastructures up on the plateau.

CONNECTION NODES between the two different methods of transport are the city's hotspots. As well as giving access to medium-distance transport, they could also have refreshment stands and pharmacies, as well as local administration and logistics offices.

As these methods of transport will circulate quite deep down inside the rock, the nodes could be natural shelters in case of emergency and could be pressurized independently from the other modules.

MAP OF THE CITY'S TRANSPORT

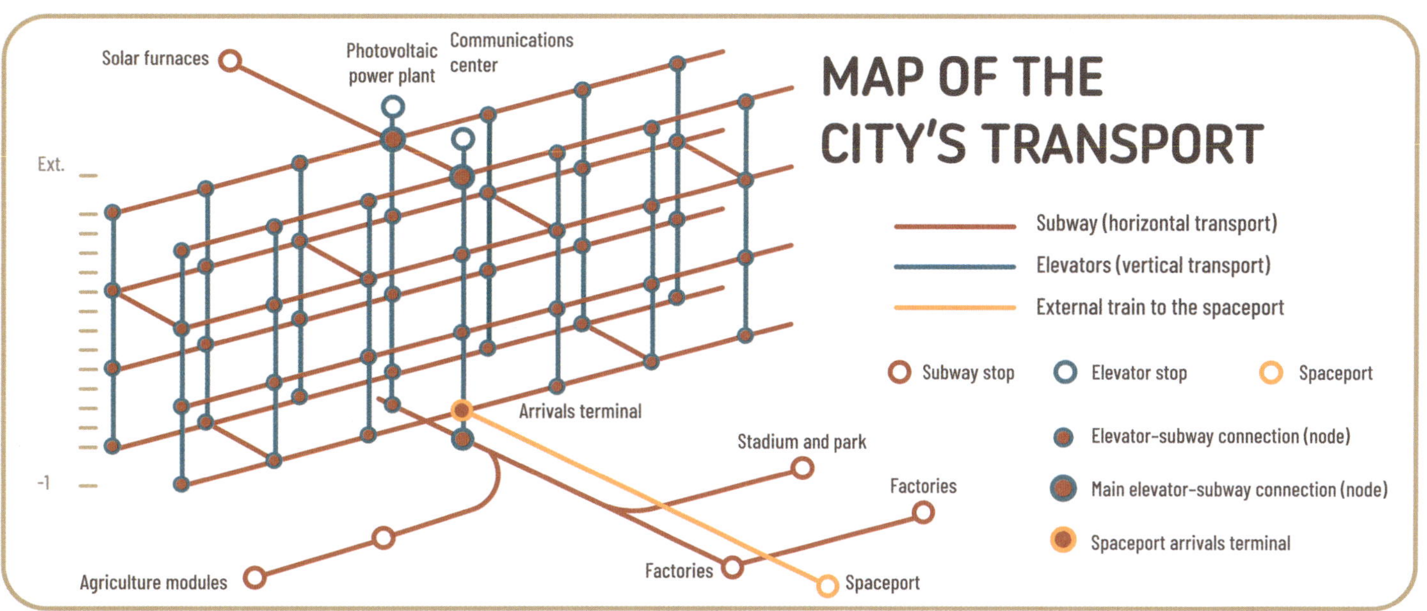

Private transport will be minimal and restricted to very light vehicles such as scooters or e-bikes.

Tunnels will need to be designed with enough space for small vehicles such as goods or emergency vehicles to use them.

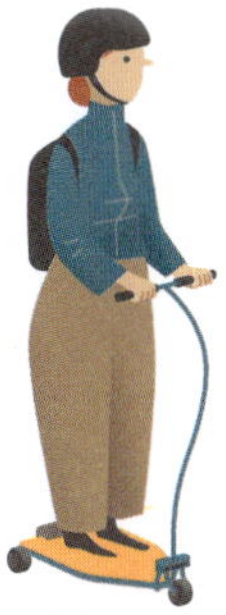

Private scooter

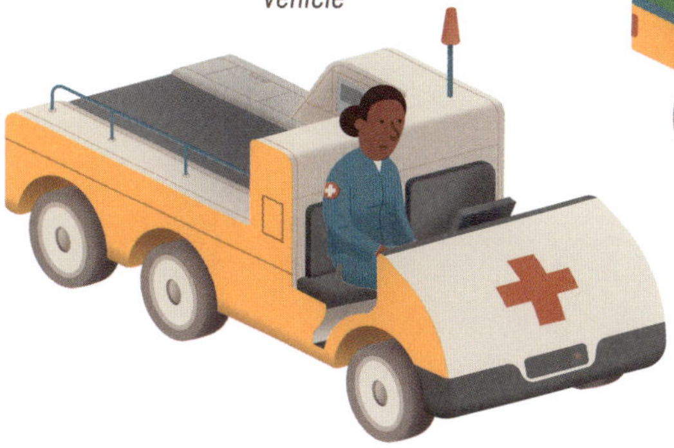

Medical emergency vehicle

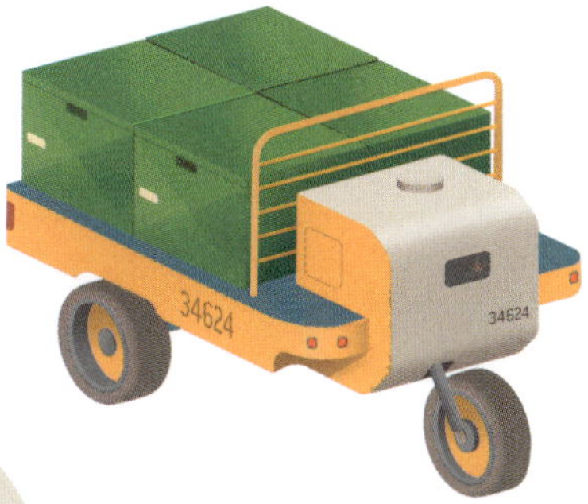

Self-driving goods vehicle

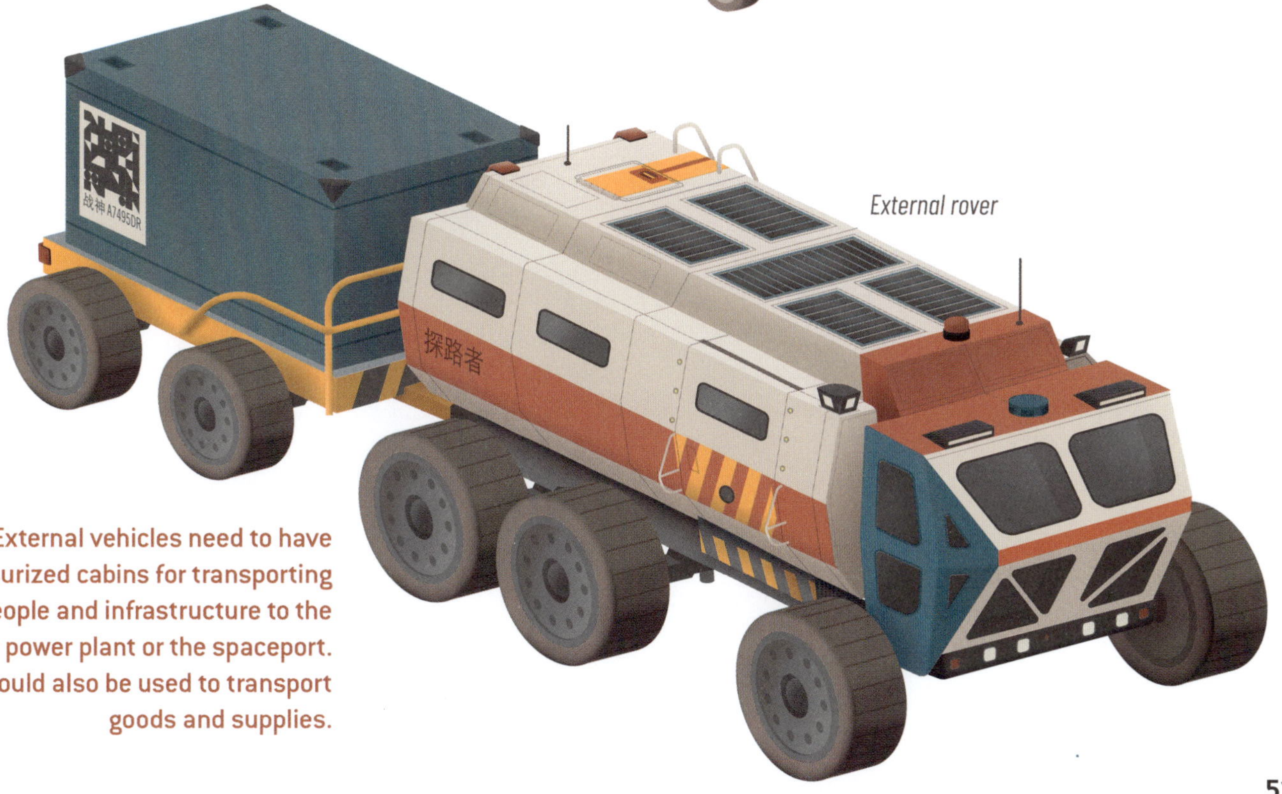

External rover

External vehicles need to have pressurized cabins for transporting people and infrastructure to the nuclear power plant or the spaceport. They would also be used to transport goods and supplies.

SOCIETY

The inhabitants of Mars will have to adapt their lifestyle to the planet's characteristics. Society will also evolve, moving away from customs on Earth to create a brand-new Martian society and culture.

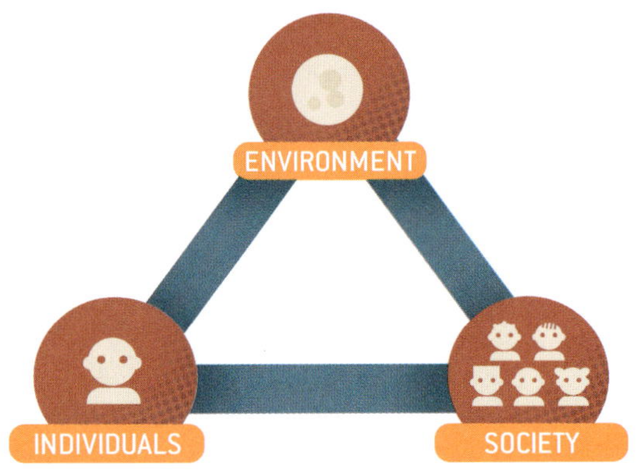

Citizens of Mars will rely heavily on their community. In such a hostile environment, people need to be able to trust the people around them, and everyone will need to contribute to make sure the group survives. Therefore, every individual needs to be encouraged to play an active role in a healthy, close-knit community.

The difficulty of extracting and processing resources on Mars will mean that radical changes will be needed in the way that people relate to the environment. Martians will be forced to adapt to their surroundings, instead of changing them. They will need to take care of the planet and use its resources sustainably.

Who will govern Mars?

Martian society and the bodies that govern it will evolve as the population grows.

Corporate phase

The inhabitants of the first bases will be scientists, engineers, and employees from private companies. They will be politically and economically dependent on decisions taken on Earth.

Semi-autonomous phase

When the first large settlements with thousands of inhabitants begin to develop, local government bodies will be created for the day-to-day running of society. However, the economy and major political decisions will continue to be controlled from Earth.

Toward independence

Once Mars has large, complex cities with a total population of more than 1,000,000 inhabitants, dependence on Earth is no longer practical. Planetary governing bodies and a new legal system will be established. At this point, the relationship and legal frameworks between Mars and Earth have to be rewritten to avoid any tension.

A new opportunity

Living on Mars will be challenging and there will be many difficulties. But it is also a unique opportunity to start over and try to learn from the mistakes made on Earth.

A Martian society based on community and respect for the environment would be a mirror in which the inhabitants of Earth could look at themselves to find solutions to many of their problems.

A community-based economy

In an environment like Mars, survival depends on access to resources and facilities in the cities: a breathable atmosphere, energy, housing, food, healthcare, etc. Therefore, all essential resources need to be owned by the community. The role of the government, with the help of artificial intelligence (AI), will be to manage them and provide them free of charge to everyone.

This does not mean that there would be no privately owned stores and businesses in the leisure, business, and non-essential services sectors.

Societies on Mars, like all societies, will develop their own artistic and cultural forms of expression. At first, these will be related to the different places on Earth the first inhabitants come from. With time, though, new languages and new forms of expression will come about, which will use the planet's own technology, resources, and environment. For this to happen, cities need to have creative spaces and access to art and culture. This will be one of the cornerstones that will forge Mars's shared identity.

TERRAFORMING

Terraforming is a process of "planetary engineering" aimed at improving a planet's environment and climate. Although the idea may seem far-fetched, it is worth remembering that human activity has already changed our world on a global scale, which has led to climate change on Earth.

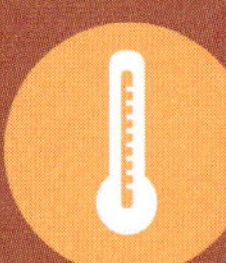

How would we "terraform" Mars ? The first thing we would have to do is heat the atmosphere. One way of doing this would be with greenhouse gases such as Mars's own carbon dioxide (CO_2), water vapor (H_2O), or more powerful gases such as perfluorocarbons.

If we manage to heat the atmosphere enough, the water frozen in the subsoil will melt and flow again. Over time, we could achieve a water cycle similar to Earth's: water evaporates, atmospheric pressure increases, and the evaporated water falls on the surface as rain. The carbon dioxide that is frozen at the poles evaporates and the atmospheric pressure rises even more, creating an atmosphere that is dense enough to heat the planet further.

The word “terraforming” refers to the concept of transforming Mars into a planet like Earth, where humans and other organisms can live.

Some scientists have suggested creating an artificial magnetic field to protect the planet from radiation. The idea is to place a magnetic dipole (an object that produces a magnetic field), as if it were a satellite, so it travels with the planet in its orbit and protects it from cosmic radiation and solar winds.

Finally, we would have to introduce oxygen (O_2) into the Martian atmosphere. In an environment without oxygen, the first native organisms could be cyanobacteria, a group of microorganisms capable of photosynthesis and releasing oxygen into the atmosphere, exactly as happened on Earth 2.4 billion years ago.

Over time, Mars would end up having an oxygen-rich atmosphere suitable for breathing. With the right temperature and pressure, liquid water on the surface, and atmospheric oxygen, Mars would have the right conditions for humans to be able to live unprotected on the surface.

Although today the idea of terraforming Mars is pure science fiction, technological improvements and advances in our civilization mean we can always dream that one day we will have another blue planet in the solar system where life can survive and thrive.

EDUARD ALTARRIBA
Designer, illustrator, and co-founder of Alababalà, a small, independent studio that offers publishing services and creates children's non-fiction publishing projects. He loves making books, games, animations, apps, and text books that are practical, educational, meaningful, and, of course, fun.

GUILLEM ANGLADA-ESCUDÉ
Researcher with a PhD in astrophysics, expert in observational astronomy, instrumentation, and the search for life beyond Earth. In 2016, he led the team that discovered Proxima b. He has worked in academic institutions in countries including the USA, Germany, the UK, and Spain. He has also worked in the field of scientific communication in collaboration with museums and international organizations.

SHEDDAD KAID-SALAH FERRÓN
Physicist and chemist who is passionate about knowledge. He delights in explaining science, especially to very young children. He writes popular science books for anyone who is curious to find out more about the world around us.

MIQUEL SUREDA ANFRES
Physicist with a PhD in aerospace engineering. He works as a university lecturer and conducts research into space exploration and sustainable planetary settlements. He spends his free time making science accessible to people of all ages through his project Gaia Ciencia.

The concept of a city on Mars and the content on pages 32–53 are inspired by the study *"The Nüwa Concept. A development model for a self-sustainable city on Mars"* available through ResearchGate DOI: 10.13140/RG.2.2.29517.56803 (Creative Commons 4.0 Attribution-only) and also published in the book *MARS CITY STATES New Societies for a New World*, 2020, published by Frank Crossman and The Mars Society. This study was led by SONet (The Sustainable Offworld Network) with contributions from Guillem Anglada-Escudé, Miquel Sureda, Gisela Detrell, Alfredo Muñoz, Owen H. Pearce, Gonzalo Rojas, Engeland Apostol, Sebastián Rodríguez, Verónica Florido, Ignasi Casanova, David Cullen, Miquel Banchs i Piqué, Philipp Hartlieb, Laia Ribas, David de la Torre, Jordi Miralda Escudé, Rafael Harillo Gomez-Pastrana, Lluís Soler Turu, Paula Betriu, Uygar Atalay, Pau Cardona, Oscar Macía, Eric Fimbinger, Stephanie Hensley, Carlos Sierra, Elena Montero, Robert Myhill, Rory Beard. Some graphic elements were inspired by the work of ABIBOO studio (https://abiboo.com/) and PEARCE+ studio.

First published 2025 in English by Button Books, an imprint of Guild of Master Craftsman Publications Ltd, Castle Place, 166 High Street, Lewes, East Sussex, BN7 1XU, UK. ISBN: 978-1-78708-158-1. Distributed by Publishers Group West in the United States. A catalog record for this book is available from the British Library. For Alababalà, Design and layout: Alababalà Studio. Editorial coordination: Meli Fernández Cela. For GMC Publications, Publisher: Jonathan Bailey. Production Director: Jim Bulley. Senior Project Editor: Tom Kitch. Design Manager: Robin Shields. Copy Editor: Claire Saunders. English Translation: Andrea Reece. Color origination by GMC Reprographics. Printed and bound in China.